THE REINS OF POWER

A CONSTITUTIONAL HISTORY OF THE UNITED STATES

The Reins of Power *is one in a group of new books dealing with American history. The purpose of these topical histories is to present in brief compass the author's interpretation of the subject. Aïda DiPace Donald is consulting editor.*

THE REINS OF POWER

A CONSTITUTIONAL HISTORY OF THE UNITED STATES

by

Bernard Schwartz

HILL AND WANG • NEW YORK

Library of Congress catalog card number: 63–19295

FIRST EDITION OCTOBER 1963

Manufactured in the United States of America
by American Book–Stratford Press, Inc.

CONTENTS

THE REINS OF POWER

A CONSTITUTIONAL HISTORY OF THE UNITED STATES

I

SEEDTIME

"LET US CONCEIVE IN OUR MIND," wrote John Wise of Massachusetts early in the eighteenth century, "a multitude of men, all naturally free and equal, going about voluntarily to erect themselves into a new commonwealth. Now their condition being such, to bring themselves into a politic body they must needs enter into diverse covenants.

"1. They must interchangeably each man covenant to join in one lasting society. . . .

"2. A vote or decree must then nextly pass to set up some particular species of government over them. . . .

"3. After a decree has specified the particular form of government, then there will be need of a new covenant, whereby those upon whom sovereignty is conferred engage to take care of the common peace and welfare; and the subjects, on the other hand, to yield them faithful obedience; in which covenant is included that submission and union of wills by which a state may be conceived."

Yet if, to our ancestors, the origins of government might thus be traced to specified contractual acts, in real life it is not that simple. The beginnings of human institutions are never quite that tidy. This is particularly true of political institutions.

Although, in one sense, the constitutional history of the United States starts definitively only with the adoption of the Federal Constitution, it is a mistake to assume that that document itself sprang Minerva-like into being, fully grown from the collective head of the Founding Fathers. Gladstone's famous contrast of the British Constitution as "the most subtle organism which has proceeded from progressive history" with the Constitution of the United States as "the most wonderful work ever struck off at a given time by the brain and purpose of man" is based upon just such an erroneous supposition. It suggests that the American Constitution is a product solely of manufacture rather than growth.

The document drafted by the men of 1787 was more than their own invention. The system drawn up by the Framers was not so much a single-stroke creation of political theorists as a codification by practical statesmen of doctrines which experience showed had worked well. The experience referred to was that of Englishmen since the Magna Charta, as well as that of the colonists themselves.

Human history, it is said, is in essence a history of ideas. If we look to the constitutional history of that country from which our institutions have sprung, we can see that it is essentially a history of the development of the idea of law as a check upon governmental power. That idea itself, to be sure, is not solely of English creation. The concept of law as a check upon arbitrary power is, on the contrary, as old as political theory itself. "He who bids the law rule," reads a noted passage from Aristotle, "bids God and reason rule, but he who bids man rule adds an element of the beast; for desire is a beast, and passion perverts rulers, even though they be the best of men. Therefore the law is reason free from desire."

Though the concept of the rule of law thus has its roots in earliest political philosophy, it remained for English constitutional history to translate it into practical reality. If, as de Tocqueville suggested, it is impossible to think of the English as living under any but a free government, it is only because they are the heirs of a successful struggle to bridle governmental power by the law of the land.

To one who looks at English constitutional history through American lenses, two names stand out: those of Coke and Locke. The contribution of John Locke is by now familiar to every American schoolboy. He it was who placed the Glorious Revolution of 1688 upon a sound doctrinal basis and, as such, furnished the philosophical justification for constitutional government, limited by fundamental organic principles. In writing as he did, Locke did not, of course, remotely dream that he was producing a handbook for American revolutionists. That is, nevertheless, precisely what he did in emphasizing that governments were limited by natural rights (including the right of the people to be taxed only with their consent) and that governments forfeited their right to exist when they ceased to respect such rights of the people. The writings of Locke furnished Americans with a basic arsenal of arguments against arbitrary rule—whether from Whitehall or Westminster.

The part played by Sir Edward Coke is not nearly so well known—except perhaps to lawyers. Yet, if anything, his contribution to the doctrinal background of the American Revolution was even more significant. Coke's views on constitutionalism were set forth, not as a matter of academic speculation, but as the law of England, by a high judicial officer of the realm. For it was as head of one of the King's courts that Coke delivered his most important pronouncements on the supremacy of the law.

Coke's most dramatic assertion of the supremacy of law occurred, in memorable circumstances, on November 13, 1608. For it was on that day that James I confronted "all the Judges of England and Barons of the Exchequer" with the claim that, since the judges were but his delegates, he could take any case he chose, remove it from the jurisdiction of the courts, and decide it in his royal person. The judges, as James saw it, were "his shadows and ministers . . . and the King may, if he please, sit and judge in Westminster Hall in any Court there and call their Judgments in question."

"To which it was answered by me," states Chief Justice Coke, "in the presence, and with the clear consent of all the Judges . . . that the King in his own person cannot adjudge any case . . . but that this ought to be determined and adjudged in some Court of Justice, according to the law and custom of England." To this, James made the shrewd reply "that he thought the law was founded upon reason, and that he and others had reason as well as the Judges."

Coke then delivered his justly celebrated answer, "that true it was, that God had endowed His Majesty with excellent science, and great endowments of nature; but His Majesty was not learned in the laws of his realm of England, and causes which concern the life, or inheritance, or goods, or fortunes of his subjects, are not to be decided by natural reason but by the artificial reason and judgment of law, which law is an act which requires long study and experience, before that a man can attain to the cognisance of it: that the law was the golden met-wand and measure to try the causes of the subjects."

It is hardly surprising that the King was, in Coke's description "greatly offended." "This means," said James, "that I shall be under the law, which it is treason to affirm." "To which," replied Coke, "I said, that Bracton saith, *quod Rex non debet esse sub homine, sed sub Deo et lege* [that the King should not be under man but under God and law]."

Needless to say, the King's anger only increased. According to one onlooker, in fact, "his Majestie fell into that high indignation as the like was never knowne in him, looking and speaking fiercely with bended fist, offering to strike him, etc."

James's indignation was well justified. Coke's articulation of the supremacy of law was utterly inconsistent with Stuart pretensions to absolute authority. In the altercation between Coke and the King, indeed, there is personified the basic conflict between power and law which underlies all political history. Nor does it affect the importance of Coke's rejection of James's claim that, with the King's fist raised against him, Coke was led personally to humble himself. That he "fell flatt on all fower" to avoid being sent to the Tower does not alter the basic boldness of his clear assertion that the law was supreme even over the Crown.

Nor did Coke stop with affirming that even the King was not above the law. In *Dr. Bonham's Case* (1610)—perhaps the most famous case decided by him—Coke seized the occasion to declare that the law was above the Parliament as well as above the King. Dr. Bonham had practiced physic without a certificate from the Royal College of Physicians. The College Censors committed him to prison, and he sued for false imprisonment. The college set forth in defense its statute of incorporation, which authorized it to regulate all physicians and punish with fine and imprisonment practitioners not admitted by it. The statute in question, however, gave the college one half of all the fines imposed. This, said Coke, made the college not only judges, but also parties, in cases coming before them, and it is an established maxim of the common law that no man may be judge in his own cause.

But what of the statute, which appeared to give the college the power to judge Dr. Bonham? Coke's answer was that even the Parliament could not confer a power so contrary to common right and reason. In his words, "it appears in our books, that in many cases, the common law will controul Acts of Parliament, and sometimes adjudge them to be utterly void: for when an Act of Parliament is against common right and reason, or repugnant, or impossible to be performed, the common law will controul it, and adjudge such Act to be void."

Modern scholars have debated over the exact meaning of these words. To the men of the formative era of American constitutional history, on the other hand, such meaning was clear. The Chief Justice of Common Pleas was stating as a rule of positive law that there was a fundamental law which limited Crown and Parliament indifferently. Had not my Lord Coke concluded that when an Act of Parliament is contrary to such fundamental law, it must be adjudged void? Did not this mean that when the British government acted toward the Colonies in a manner contrary to common right and reason, its decrees were of no legal force?

The men of the American Revolution were nurtured upon Coke's writings. "Coke's *Institutes,*" wrote John Rutledge of South Carolina, "seem to be almost the foundation of our law." Modern writers may characterize Coke as an obsolete writer whom the British Constitution has outgrown. Americans of the eighteenth century did not have the benefit of such ex post facto criticism. To them, Coke was the contemporary colossus of the law—"our juvenile oracle," John Adams termed him in an 1816 letter—who combined in his own person the positions of highest judge, commentator on the law, and leader of the parliamentary opposition to Stuart tyranny. Coke's famous *Commentary upon Littleton,* said Jefferson, "was the universal elementary book of law students and a sounder Whig never wrote nor of profounder learning in the orthodox doctrines of . . . British liberties." When Coke, after affirming the supremacy of the law to royal prerogative, announced, "It is not I, Edward Coke, that speaks it but the records that speak it," men on the western side of the Atlantic took his assertion that he was only declaring, not making, law as the literal truth.

Edmund Burke has attested to the extent of legal education in the American Colonies. "In no country perhaps in the world," he declared in his *Second Speech on Conciliation with America,* "is the law so general a study." Such study, he went on, "renders men inquisitive, dexterous, prompt in attack, ready in defence, full of resources. . . . They augur misgovernment at a distance, and snuff the approach of tyranny in every tainted breeze." To such men, Coke's contribution was a fundamental one. He stated the supremacy of law in terms of positive law. And it was in such terms that the doctrine was of such import to the Founders of the American Republic. When they spoke of a government of laws and not of men, they were not indulging in mere rhetorical flourish.

The influence of Coke may be seen at all of the key stages in the development of the conflict between the Colonies and the mother country. From Whitehall Palace, to which King James had summoned the judges in 1608, to the Council Chamber of the Boston Town House a century and a half later was not really so far as it seemed. "That council chamber," wrote John Adams over half a century after the event, "was as respectable an apartment as the House of Commons or the House of Lords in Great Britain. . . . In this chamber, round a great fire, were seated five Judges, with Lieutenant Governor Hutchinson at their head, as Chief Justice, all arrayed in their new, fresh, rich robes of scarlet

English broadcloth; in their large cambric bands, and immense judicial wigs." For it was in this chamber that, in 1761, James Otis delivered his landmark attack in *Paxton's Case* against general writs of assistance.

The Otis argument in *Paxton's Case* has been characterized as the opening gun of the controversy leading to the Revolution. In it, Otis with "a torrent of impetuous eloquence . . . hurried away everything before him." He argued the cause, Otis declared, "with the greater pleasure . . . as it is in opposition to a kind of power, the exercise of which, in former periods of English history, cost one King of England his head, and another his throne." If Patrick Henry came close to treason in his famous speech of 1765, he at least had an excellent model in this Otis speech.

To demonstrate the illegality of the writs of assistance, Otis went straight back to Coke. As Horace Gray (later a Justice of the Supreme Court) put it in an 1865 comment, "His main reliance was the well-known statement of Lord Coke in *Dr. Bonham's Case*." This may be seen clearly from John Adams' summary of the Otis argument: "As to acts of Parliament. An act against the Constitution is void: an Act against natural Equity is void: and if an Act of Parliament should be made in the very words of the petition, it would be void. The . . . Courts must pass such Acts into disuse."

The Otis oration, exclaimed Adams, "breathed into this nation the breath of life," and, "Then and there the child Independence was born." To which we may add, with Edward S. Corwin, that then and there American constitutional law was born. For Otis, in Justice Gray's words, "denied that [Parliament] was the final arbiter of the justice and constitutionality of its own acts; and . . . contended that the validity of statutes must be judged by the courts of justice; and thus foreshadowed the principle of American constitutional law, that it is the duty of the judiciary to declare unconstitutional statutes void."

Coke's biographer tells us that he would have been astonished at the uses to which *Dr. Bonham's Case* was put. Certain it is that Otis and those who followed in his steps went far beyond anything the great English jurist had expressly intended. Yet had not

Coke's own attitude been stated in his picturesque phrase: "Let us now peruse our ancient authors, for out of the old fields must come the new corne"? That is precisely what Americans have done in using Coke as the foundation for the constitutional edifice which, starting with Otis' argument, they have erected. Coke himself would not have been disturbed by the fact that, though the fields were old, the corn was new.

It was in the controversy over the Stamp Act, however, that Coke's influence had its most important American results. As already noted, John Adams attributed the honor of starting the nation on the road to independence to Otis. In 1776, on the other hand, he had stated that the "author of the first Virginia Resolutions against the stamp act . . . will have the glory with posterity, of beginning . . . this great Revolution."

On May 29, 1765, Patrick Henry sprang to the fore in the Virginia House of Burgesses, while that assembly was considering the newly enacted Stamp Act. It was known that Mr. Henry was not really learned in the law (he had, indeed, been admitted to the bar after six weeks' study of only Coke and the Virginia Statutes). Yet he had read in *Coke upon Littleton* that an Act of Parliament against the Magna Charta, or common right, or reason was void. And it was on the flyleaf of his old copy of that book that the unlearned young lawyer wrote out a set of resolutions protesting against the Stamp Act. It was these resolutions which Henry presented to the Virginia assembly, together with the "treasonable" speech with which his name has forever remained associated. Young Thomas Jefferson, who witnessed the scene, later recalled how "torrents of sublime eloquence from Mr. Henry . . . prevailed" to secure passage of most of the resolutions.

Throughout the Colonies, the Stamp Act was opposed on the same ground that Otis had urged in *Paxton's Case.* John Adams used the Otis argument in presenting a petition "that the Stamp Act was null because unconstitutional" to the Governor and Council of Massachusetts, and a committee of the legislative assembly of that colony resolved that business should be done without stamps. The "prevailing reason" given for their resolve, as well as the action of the people in following it, according to Thomas

Hutchinson, then Lieutenant Governor of Massachusetts, was "that the Act of Parliament is against Magna Carta and the natural rights of Englishmen, and therefore according to Lord Coke null and void."

Even the judges appointed by the royal governors were not prepared to deny this principle. Justice William Cushing, a member of the highest Massachusetts bench, in a letter, dated "In a hurry Feby. 7, 1766," to Lieutenant Governor Hutchinson (who was then also Chief Justice of Massachusetts), wrote, "Its true It is said an Act of Parliament against natural Equity is void." That being the case, "If we admit evidence unstamped . . . Q. if it can be said we do wrong." Later, his opinion more settled, Cushing could write to John Adams, "I can tell the grand jury the nullity of Acts of Parliament."

The Virginia judges went even further, for a court in that colony actually ruled, in February, 1766, that the Stamp Act was void. The judges "unanimously declared it to be their opinion," we are told in a contemporary account, "that the said act did not bind, affect, or concern the inhabitants of this colony inasmuch as they conceive the same to be unconstitutional."

Men whose education had been, in large part, based upon Coke quite naturally gave a legal turn to their disaffection with the Stamp Act. "Our friends to liberty," wrote Thomas Hutchinson during the heat of the Stamp Act controversy, "take the advantage of a maxim they find in Lord Coke that an Act of Parliament against Magna Carta or the peculiar rights of Englishmen is ipso facto void." This, Hutchinson went on, is what "seems to have determined a great part of the colony to oppose the execution of the act with force."

Interestingly enough, the colonists not only relied upon Coke's authority in arguing the invalidity of the Stamp Act. They also followed his example when he was a leader of the last Parliament in which he sat—that of 1628. In the two years which had intervened since the dissolution of the prior Parliament, Englishmen had suffered serious attacks upon their personal liberties, far graver, in fact, than those to which the Colonies were later to be subjected. The members of the House of Commons were confronted with the basic question of what they should do about the situation. Coke it was who, weighted with age and prestige (that great *"Monarcha Juris,"* John Selden had termed him in that Parliament), rose to declare that it was the law of the realm that counted, not mere gracious promises from the throne. "Messages of love," he urged, "never came into a Parliament. Let us put up a Petition of Right! Not that I distrust the King; but that I cannot take his trust but in a Parliamentary way." The result was the landmark Petition of Right—enacted as a law—declaring the fundamental rights of Englishmen.

When the colonists, in response to the Stamp Act crisis, met in intercolonial congress to deal with the situation, they, too, acted through a measure declaring the rights of Englishmen, as these were conceived to apply in the American Colonies. The Declaration of Rights and Grievances passed by the Stamp Act Congress, declaring "the most essential rights and liberties of the colonists, and of the grievances under which they labour, by reason of several late acts of parliament," was a natural response of men familiar with the constitutional history of Stuart England. The 1765 declaration was the direct descendant of the Petition of Right.

In time of constitutional crisis, all the same, declaratory enactment alone is hardly adequate to halt the ultimate resort to more forceful measures. The declaration of 1765, like its 1628 predecessor, had to be implemented by cannon and marching feet before its principles were to be of more than only hortatory effect.

Before we can discuss the later stages of the conflict with Britain, however, a word must be said about the earlier history of the Colonies. As already pointed out, it was Locke and Coke who furnished the colonists with the doctrinal basis for their resistance to the claims of the mother country. But mere legal argument is not enough to make a revolution. The colonists could turn the Coke-Locke philosophy to their ends only because their prior history had brought them to a stage where they were able to do so.

The most important thing to bear in mind, in considering the constitutional history of the American Colonies, is that it is a history of *British* colonies. From a constitutional point of view, the

Colonies settled by Great Britain were unique—utterly unlike those of Spain or France or the nations of antiquity. When Englishmen migrated they took with them, in the words of a parliamentary debate, "all of the first great privileges of Englishmen on their backs." Let an Englishman go where he would, said the counsel to the Board of Trade in 1720, in lands claimed by England, he carried as much of law and liberty with him as the nature of things would bear. It was because of this that Patrick Henry could claim, in the first of his resolves passed by the Virginia assembly, that the people of that colony possessed "all the Liberties, Privileges, Franchises and Immunities that at any Time have been held, enjoyed and possessed by the People of Great Britain." A similar claim could hardly have been asserted by Frenchmen, Spaniards, or Romans who settled overseas.

According to Thomas Pownall, perhaps the best of the Massachusetts colonial governors, the rights of Englishmen were preserved to the American colonists because of the fact that the Island of Jersey had, by its constitution, "a shadow and semblance of an English parliament." This precedent, he said, made it easy to put the same idea into early American charters. Certainly, the colonial charters played an important part in the constitutional training of Americans. The grant of the charters themselves was a natural development in an age when grants of property, powers, and immunities were commonly made through such instruments. When the first colonists came to Virginia, they came armed with a charter granted by James I, on April 10, 1606, authorizing them "to make Habitation, Plantation, and to deduce a Colony of sundry of our People into that part of *America,* commonly called VIRGINIA." This charter called for the setting up of local government and expressly reserved to those who should live in the new Colony "all Liberties, Franchises, and Immunities . . . to all Intents and Purposes, as if they had been abiding and born, within this our Realm of *England.*"

Along with the charters went the policy of establishing representative institutions in the Colonies. "For in the Governments, where there are Charters," wrote Jeremiah Dummer in his early eighteenth-century *Defence of the New England Charters,*

". . . all Officers Civil and Military are elected by the People." This was to overstate the extent of popular control, but it is a fact that local legislatures did quickly develop in all of the colonies. The Virginia colony was in existence little over a decade when London ordered the setting up of a representative assembly, the House of Burgesses, whose members were duly chosen in 1619.

A similar development occurred as the other Colonies came to be settled—either, as in the case of Virginia, through decrees from London or through the voluntary action of the colonists themselves. The outstanding example of the latter type was the system of representative government established in 1639 by the emigrants from Massachusetts who founded the towns of Windsor, Hartford, and Wethersfield on the Connecticut River. The *Fundamental Orders of Connecticut,* which they drew up, deserves its characterization by C. H. Van Tyne as "the first written constitution known to history that created a government." The *Orders* provided for a general assembly composed of representatives chosen from the different towns, and for a governor and other officers to be elected annually.

Almost from the beginning, then, the colonists became endowed with the two essentials of the English Constitution: a representative legislative assembly and a recognition of the basic rights of Englishmen. More than that, the establishment of such essentials in written fundamental laws like the Connecticut *Orders,* or documents in the form of charters granted from London, had a profound influence on American constitutional ideas.

It may be true that, from a strictly legal point of view, all such colonial organic instruments hardly possessed anything like the status attained by later American constitutions. The charters received from London were accorded as a matter of privilege and grace. They could be amended or revoked at the will of the grantor. The charters may, in fact, as Charles McIlwain has pointed out, have become free constitutions in America. Yet, in law, they remained only medieval grants. In law, they continued subject to the will of the grantor, though they regulated the lives and property of ever-increasing thousands of Americans.

The same was clearly true—with regard to control from London—of the fundamental laws, like the Connecticut *Orders,* drawn up by the colonists themselves. These, too, were legally subject to the overriding authority of the British government. So far as the law was concerned, then, the charters and fundamental laws of the Colonies were weak bulwarks behind which to defend the rights of Americans against the mother country. In the law, there was no answer to Lord Mansfield's assertion that the American governments set up by charter were "all on the same footing as our great corporations in London."

More important, nevertheless, than the letter of the law with regard to the colonial charters was the manner in which those instruments were viewed by the bulk of Americans. "Who, then," asked John Adams in 1818, "was the author, inventor, discoverer of independence? The only true answer must be the first emigrants, and the proof of it is the charter of James I." The strict legal rule might make of the charters mere matters of royal grace. But the colonists looked upon them as much more. The very first charter, that of James I to Virginia, said Adams, "is more like a treaty between independent sovereigns than like a charter or grant of privileges from a sovereign to his subjects."

Americans looked upon their charters as the written source of their basic institutions and freedoms and were quick to oppose any infringements upon their charter rights. As early as 1664, the men of Massachusetts resisted an attempt to replace their charter by commissioners sent from London to "regulate" New England. The colonists, we are told, put their charter in safe hands, manned the harbor fort, and petitioned the King to let their "laws and liberties live." When, in 1681, their charter rights were again attacked, they asserted that it was their undoubted duty "to abide by what rights and privileges the Lord our God in his merciful providence hath bestowed upon us."

In 1684, to be sure, the Massachusetts charter was actually withdrawn and the Dominion of New England governed in accordance with Sir Edmund Andros' notions of Stuart prerogative. But the resistance of the colonists led to the granting of a new charter in 1691. In the other Colonies, the situation was similar.

The charters were regarded as the fundamental basis of rights and liberties. When the charters were restricted or modified, the colonists, it has been said, felt the loss as Englishmen might have mourned the loss of the Magna Charta. The attachment to the charters continued until almost the end of the colonial period. When the Massachusetts judges were impeached by that colony's House of Representatives in 1774, they were charged with "high crimes and misdemeanors, and . . . a conspiracy against the charter liberties of the people."

Just as significant as the way in which the colonists conceived of their charters was the training in self-government which they received in operating the institutions provided for under those instruments. "Englishmen hate an arbitrary power," wrote John Wise in 1710, ". . . as they hate the devil." The political history of the Colonies shows that such hatred was not diminished among those Englishmen who had migrated to North America.

From the beginning of their existence, the colonial legislatures looked upon themselves as the direct descendants of the House of Commons, vested with the privileges and powers won by that body in its struggle against executive absolutism. This was apparent at the very first sitting of the first colonial assembly, the Virginia House of Burgesses. When the Speaker took exception to the qualifications of two members, the House, in direct imitation of the English Commons, proceeded to exercise the right to judge the qualifications of its own members.

In many ways, the constitutional history of the Colonies in the century before the Revolution was a miniature copy of that which had occurred in seventeenth-century England. The claim for which one Stuart king lost his life and another his throne was put forward in lesser form by the royal governors. The result was constant conflict between the popular assemblies and the governors. Although the governors themselves were in the main hardly the "men of vicious characters" described by Franklin, they were direct agents of the prerogative, with commissions and instructions which made them autocrats not beholden to those whom they governed. In England itself, the prerogative had been completely bridled by the revolutions which overthrew Stuart tyranny. In the Colonies, on the other hand, the royal prerogative continued, in theory at least, without diminution, and the governors were expected to be agents of Whitehall's will. It was inevitable that such agents would be opposed by the provincial assemblies—the articulate organs of men who, in Clinton Rossiter's phrase, were "more English than the English in their obstinacy, pride, and hypersensitivity in matters of self-government."

It might be more accurate to say that, from a constitutional point of view, the colonists remained more Englishmen of the seventeenth century than those of the eighteenth century. In England, the seventeenth century was the great age of struggle against government by prerogative. That struggle was definitively concluded with the final expulsion of the Stuart kings. Thenceforth, the English executive was to be completely subordinate to the representatives of the people.

In North America at the same time, the basic contention between the legislative and executive branches continued, for the blessings which 1688 brought to the mother country (so signally commemorated in Locke's writings) were not extended across the Atlantic. If anything, indeed, as we shall see, the establishment of parliamentary supremacy, with the accession of William and Mary, was to make a sharpening of the constitutional conflict in the Colonies inevitable.

Looked at in this manner, it is not mere hyperbole to characterize the constitutional history of the Colonies as a chapter torn from the constitutional history of Stuart England. The battles between Crown and Parliament were all fought out, on a smaller scale, on the western side of the Atlantic. And, in America, too, the theme was that of gradual triumph of the popular assembly. Many of Parliament's hard-won privileges—control over its own procedure, freedom of debate, determination of election disputes and the qualifications of members—were also secured by the colonial legislatures. Even more important was the successful assertion by the assemblies of that power which was the very keystone of the arch of parliamentary authority itself, namely, the power of the purse. That power alone, coupled as it was with the failure of the British government to provide a permanent civil list in any of the Colonies (in most Colonies, the salary of the governor himself had become dependent upon appropriations by the local legislature), led to the dominance of the assemblies in most colonial governments by the end of the French and Indian War.

Had the mother country continued to treat the Colonies with "a wise and salutary neglect," it is possible that colonial institutions would have taken their own way to the "perfection" of which Burke speaks—thereby anticipating by a century the modern development of the British Commonwealth. Such peaceful development within the British Empire was, however, made impossible with the assertion by London of an entirely new theory of imperial power after the successful expulsion of the French from North America. It is in this sense that there is constitutional truth in Francis Parkman's well-known statement, "With the fall of Quebec began the history of the United States."

The establishment of parliamentary supremacy, with the final overthrow of the Stuart kings, as already intimated, brought on a constitutional clash with the Colonies that was well-nigh unavoidable. When William and Mary came to the throne, they swore to govern the kingdom "and the dominions thereunto belonging according to the statutes in Parliament agreed on." Having emerged wholly victorious from its struggle with the Crown, it was scarcely to be expected that the supreme legislature would forbear to exercise its hard-won prerogatives over any portion of the British dominions. So far as the Colonies were concerned, in truth, the divine right of kings had been succeeded by the divine right of Parliament. As an American newspaper put it, Parliament was displaying "a kingly fondness for prerogative." It was, as John C. Miller points out, the refusal of Americans to bow before the new divinity that precipitated the American Revolution.

It was not until the close of the French and Indian War and the Stamp Act and other imperial legislation resulting from that conflict that the Americans felt the full weight of the new theory of parliamentary divinity. By the middle of the eighteenth century, Englishmen and Americans held altogether different notions about the constitutional nature of the British Empire. In Britain itself, the dominant principle, established since 1688, was that of the unrestricted legal supremacy of the Parliament over all British dominions—exemplified in de Lolme's celebrated maxim that Parliament can do everything except make a woman a man, and a man a woman. Americans of the mid-eighteenth century were scarcely disposed to acknowledge such absolute authority in the British legislature.

It should not be forgotten that the Glorious Revolution of 1688 was a real revolution in the constitutional sense. It rendered constitutional and legitimate for the realm what had theretofore been considered as revolutionary. The British Constitution had, in other words, been drastically changed through the people's right of revolution. Such change had not, however, been equally recognized on the western side of the Atlantic. "The authority of parliament," declared John Adams in his *Novanglus* letters, "was never generally acknowledged in America." The colonists could contend that what was revolutionary in Britain in 1688 remained such, until assented to, outside Britain itself. Hence, in McIlwain's characterization, the absolute power of Parliament, new and revolutionary in England in 1688, was for the Colonies still revolutionary three quarters of a century later.

The conflict which led to the American Revolution was, at least in its origins, in large part a conflict over different interpretations of the British Constitution. "In Britain," wrote Governor Bernard of Massachusetts in 1765, "the American Governments are considered as Corporations empowered to make by-Laws, existing only during the Pleasure of Parliament. . . . In America they claim . . . to be perfect States, no otherwise dependent upon Great Britain than by having the same King."

Here, then, was the legal nub of the constitutional controversy that divided the Colonies from the mother country. The Parliament, recognized as supreme in Britain for almost a century, impelled by the needs of empire, sought to extend its sway, in practice as well as theory, to the overseas dominions belonging to the realm. The Colonies, whose own institutions of self-government had grown all but to maturity, denied that they were subject to the unlimited control of a legislature in which they had no direct voice. In effect, the Americans were asserting a dominion status within a British Commonwealth a century before the mother country was ready to recognize such status.

The colonists considered themselves the direct heirs of those Englishmen who had met and mastered the first Stuart efforts at absolutism. Having successfully contended with their local executives during the century following the deposition of Charles I, it was not to be expected that Americans would readily give up their rights of self-government. To the colonists, they were continuing the tradition of the Long Parliament against that body which had inherited Stuart pretensions to absolute prerogative. It is in this sense that we may agree with the conclusion of one historian that, in the American Revolution, the England of the seventeenth century met and prevailed against the England of the eighteenth century.

The encounter between the two theories of the British Constitution was one which could scarcely be resolved by compromise between the diametrically opposed English and American viewpoints. While London was willing to revoke exactions like the Stamp Act which were obnoxious to the colonists (although these were revoked more because of their harmful effect on British, rather than American, interests), it could not give way on its constitutional right to legislate for the Colonies without yielding on the essentials to the American view. Thus, although the Stamp Act was repealed, its repeal was accompanied by the Declaratory Act, which categorically asserted that Parliament "had, hath, and of right ought to have, full power and authority to make such laws and statutes of sufficient force and validity to bind the colonies and people of America . . . in all cases whatsoever."

On their side, the Americans, overjoyed though they doubtless were over repeal, could hardly acquiesce in "the peppercorn, in acknowledgment of the right," without conceding the correctness of the parliamentary interpretation of the British Constitution. The American position was acutely stated by

Franklin during his questioning in 1766 by a committee of the House of Commons. He was asked whether, if the Stamp Act were repealed, it would induce the American assemblies to acknowledge the right of Parliament to tax them and to erase their resolutions against the Stamp Act. "No, never," was his reply. His questioner went on, "Is there no means of obliging them to erase those resolutions?" "None that I know of," answered the good Doctor, "they will never do it unless compelled by force of arms."

Within less than a decade, of course, there came precisely that attempt through British arms to compel the Americans to renounce their claims. Once both sides became publicly committed to their constitutional positions, the situation really became that stated by George III in 1774: "The die is cast. The colonists must either triumph or submit."

The issue was no longer whether the colonists were to be taxed for their own defense. That being the case, it did not matter that the amounts involved were in fact quite small or even that, in the case of the tea tax, the end result would be a cheaper price for American consumers. It may well be, as McIlwain has pointed out, that the colonists stood no greater risk of actual impoverishment than Hampden did when he refused Charles I's demand for payment of Ship Money. But both Hampden and the Americans were sincerely convinced that their constitutional rights were being violated and that acquiescence on their part would have the most disastrous consequences. By the eve of the Revolution, the basic question had become whether the principle of the Declaratory Act was to be the rule governing the relations between the Colonies and the mother country. And, when it came to that, as Franklin had foreseen ten years earlier, the question could only be answered by the force of arms.

II

FRUITION

"THE BLESSINGS OF SOCIETY," wrote John Adams in 1776, "depend entirely on the constitutions of government." Hence, it was only natural that the men of the Revolution should turn to constitution-making when once the conflict with Britain reached the stage where independence was the only real alternative to submission. Full separation from the mother country made necessary a new governmental structure in the Colonies, which were thenceforth to be free states absolved from allegiance to the British Crown.

While British governors were being driven from power or fleeing in the face of popular feeling, civil government had to be carried on; a new legal basis had to be provided for that which had been forcibly dissolved. The problem confronting the colonists is shown by the experience of New Hampshire, the first colony to draw up its own system of independent self-government. At the beginning of 1776, the Congress of that colony declared:

> The sudden and abrupt departure of . . . our late Governor and several of the Council, leaving us destitute of Legislation; and no Executive Courts being open to punish criminal offenders, whereby the lives and properties of the honest people of the Colony, are

> liable to the machinations and evil designs of wicked men: Therefore, for the preservation of peace and good order, and for the security of the lives and properties of the inhabitants of this Colony, we conceive ourselves reduced to the necessity of establishing a form of Government.

The establishment of governments to meet the vacuum caused by the elimination of the royal governments was treated at first as only a temporary expedient—intended, in the words of the New Hampshire Congress, "to continue during the present unhappy and unnatural contest." It was soon seen, however, that something more formal and abiding was necessary. "Each colony," John Adams wrote in March, 1776, "should establish its own government and then a league should be formed between them all." And, two months later, the Second Continental Congress adopted a resolution calling for the full exercise of local government and the suppression of all royal authority and urging the various Colonies to set up governments of their own. Adams termed this "the most important Resolution that ever was taken in America." Though Adams sometimes overdid his use of superlatives, this characterization was not too wide of the mark.

The May, 1776, resolution had two vital consequences: the one practical, the other constitutional. In the first place, it meant (as Adams himself emphasized at the time) virtual independence. The call for the Colonies to convert themselves into states, with governments of their own, meant that they were, in Jefferson's phrase, "matured for falling from the parent stem." In this sense, the May resolution signalized the effective separation from the mother country and rendered inevitable its formal declaration on July 4.

Of perhaps equal importance is what the congressional resolution of May, 1776, tells us about a key constitutional problem which has plagued the American Union ever since its creation. This problem has been termed the greatest of all the questions left unresolved by the Founders: the nation-state relationship.

"The Constitution," declared Justice Douglas in a 1946 opinion, "is a compact between sovereigns." In this view, the Union was formed by the voluntary league of thirteen independent sovereigns. This is the notion of state sovereignty which has been the principal reliance of all those who, from the founding of the Republic, have sought to weaken the national structure created by the Framers. But the May, 1776, resolution of the Continental Congress indicates dramatically that the notion of state sovereignty has never had a valid *legal* basis. Before the Revolution, of course, the states were only colonies, with sovereignty over them vested in the British Crown. It is, nevertheless, erroneous to assume that the Declaration of Independence transformed them into thirteen fully grown sovereign states. "Was then the American revolution effected . . . ," asks Madison in *The Federalist,* "was the precious blood of thousands spilt, and the hard-earned substance of millions lavished, not that the people of America should enjoy peace, liberty, and safety; but that the governments of the individual states . . . might . . . be arrayed with certain dignities and attributes of sovereignty?"

On the contrary, as the Supreme Court said in a 1936 case, when "the external sovereignty of Great Britain in respect of the colonies ceased, it immediately passed to the Union." The Union of the Colonies, indeed, preceded the Declaration of Independence, which was itself a joint act. The Union is thus, in the words of Lincoln's First Inaugural Address, "much older than the Constitution. It was formed, in fact, by the Articles of Association in 1774. It was matured and continued by the Declaration of Independence."

It was because of this that Lincoln could rightly make his oft-quoted statement that the states have their status in the Union, and that they have no other legal status. That this is true is shown by the fact that it was the organ of the nation that called the state governments into being. The states had no formal legal existence until the Congress recommended to them, in Adams' phrase, "to abolish all authority under the crown, and institute and organize a new government, under the authority of the people." It was only when the different Colonies, acting pursuant to the congressional resolution, established their own systems of government that they were legally transformed into the states which made up the American confederation.

Hence, as Lincoln put it in his First Message to Congress, "The Union is older than any of the States, and in fact it created them as States. . . . Not one of them ever had a State Constitution independent of the Union." To speak of such bodies as independent sovereigns is to use Humpty Dumpty's method of making words mean "just what I choose it to mean—neither more nor less."

Effect was given to the congressional resolution of May, 1776, by the drawing up of constitutions establishing the new governments which had been called for. By the end of the Revolution, written constitutions had been adopted in all the states. Eleven of these were wholly new documents, while two of them, those of Connecticut and Rhode Island, were essentially the old royal charters with minor modifications.

"A constitution in the American sense of the word," we are informed by Justice Samuel Miller's classic definition, "is a written instrument by which the fundamental powers of the government are established, limited, and defined, and by which these powers are distributed among several departments, for their more safe and useful exercise, for the benefit of the body politic." The state constitutions drafted during the Revolution were the first organic instruments in this country which may truly be termed constitutions in this sense. They were written documents drawn up by men trained in the law, under which governmental powers were both conferred and limited. The polity set up by them was dominated by the separation of powers, composed as it was of three distinct departments, though emphasizing the primacy of the elected legislature. This was a natural development—the fruit of the colonists' contention with the royal governors.

As Esmond Wright has put it, the first state constitutions were soundly based on colonial experience and in this sense were evolutionary, not revolutionary. The drafting of written basic documents was the natural response to be expected from men who were themselves the products of colonial constitutional history, when they received the call of the Continental Congress to set up governments of their own. Clinton Rossiter has gone further and asserted that the men of the Revolution, in a sense, really had no choice in the matter: "The colonial heritage, the recent frustrations of defending an unwritten constitution against parliamentary intrusion, the withdrawal of viceregal power and consequent demand for new organs of government—all these factors made the Revolutionary constitutions an inevitable next step in the progress of political liberty."

This is a most acute observation, if not carried to a deterministic extreme. If we summarize colonial constitutional experience, the concept of fundamental law contained in charters and other basic documents stands out. It was by appeal to such fundamental law that the rights of the colonists as Englishmen were asserted. It was because of the existence of such fundamental law that the colonists were able to develop their own institutions of self-government. And, it should never be forgotten, it was Parliament's violation of the colonists' right to self-government that, more than anything else, was the direct cause of the Revolution. Charles Warren, the noted legal historian, tells of the 1837 interview of a veteran of the War for Independence, who, when questioned whether the cause of the taking up of arms was the Stamp Act, the tea tax, or "the eternal principles of liberty," replied that they were all of no real importance. Well, then, he was asked, why did he fight? "Young man," was the answer, "what we meant in going for the red-coats was this: we always had governed ourselves and we always meant to. They didn't mean we should."

The colonial right to self-government was, however, as already emphasized, constantly subjected to challenge by the royal governors. During the century-long friction between the governors and the legislative assemblies, the appeal to fundamental law—whether in the charters or the principles of the British Constitution—became a major weapon of the colonists. But they could readily see how much weaker their claims were when they were based upon unwritten principles than they would have been had they been articulated in a written higher law which men had to live by. It was consequently logical for them to develop the slogan "a government of laws and not of men." By the time of the Revolution, Americans firmly believed that government should be operated only by men whose status, duties, and powers were firmly fixed in specific fundamental laws. As a colonist wrote in 1771, though "we are all rogues, there must be Law, and all we want is to be governed by Law, and not by the Will of Officers, which to us is perfectly despotick and arbitrary."

The first state constitutions were a direct result of the belief just discussed. The colonists had become sorely aware of the lack of higher laws which were legally, as well as morally, beyond the reach of those who exercised governmental power. When the time came, they sought to correct the deficiency with binding written directions.

Almost all of the state constitutions drawn up in response to the congressional resolution of May, 1776, were drafted and adopted within a few months. Securing an organic document for the Union proved to be a more difficult matter. As early as July, 1775, Franklin (himself the author of the Albany Plan for intercolonial union) had submitted to the Continental Congress a draft of Articles of Confederation and Perpetual Union. No action was taken on this proposal. A year later, after Richard Henry Lee moved his resolution in favor of a Declaration of Independence, he also offered a second one proposing a committee "to prepare and digest the form of a confederation to be entered into between these colonies." The committee appointed to give effect to such resolution, with John Dickinson as its chairman, proceeded on the basis of the Franklin draft. Its work resulted in the Articles of Confederation, adopted by the Congress during the autumn of 1777, though not approved by all of the states until 1781, when they finally went into effect.

George Kennan has recently pointed out, "Coalitions find it possible to agree, as a rule, only on what *not* to do. This is the reason why their tendency is so often to do nothing at all." The united Colonies could act effectively to end the connection with the mother country, for they could decide unanimously that they did not want to be governed by Britain. When it came to deciding upon the details of a more permanent union, at the same time, there was not the same accord. On the contrary, the drafting of an instrument of Union brought to the fore the interstate and intersectional differences, which even the needs of war for independence had not fully suppressed. That being the case, it is scarcely surprising that the Articles of Confederation themselves failed to provide for a Union endowed with the full authority needed to render it effective.

The polity provided for by the Articles was strikingly different from that set up in the various state constitutions. As already indicated, the state constitutions had been based on a strict separation of powers. The Articles, on the other hand, concentrated all the governmental authority provided for under it in a unicameral legislative body. As Justice William Paterson explained it in a 1795 case, "Congress was the general, supreme, and controlling council of the nation, the centre of union, the centre of force, and the sun of the political system."

The concentration of all the authority of the Union in the Congress was, nevertheless, more than offset by the absence of the requisites of effective national power. The lack in this respect was pointed out in a 1786 article:

> By this political compact the United States in congress have exclusive power for the following purposes, without being able to execute one of them. They may make and conclude treaties; but can only recommend the observance of them. They may appoint ambassadors; but cannot defray even the expenses of their tables. They may borrow money in their own name on the faith of the Union; but cannot pay a dollar. They may coin money; but they cannot purchase an ounce of bullion. They may make war, and determine what number of troops are necessary; but cannot raise a single soldier. *In short, they may declare every thing, but do nothing.*

The government established in 1781 was vested with important powers, but it suffered from two fundamental defects. The first of these stemmed from the fact that the authority of the

Confederation did not rest directly on the people of the nation. The Congress was composed of delegates chosen and paid by the state legislatures and each state had one vote. The second defect flowed naturally from the first. It was the lack of effective coercive authority in the Union. Since the authority of the Confederation Congress did not extend to individual citizens of the different states, its measures could only become operative through implementation by the states themselves. There was no national compulsive power to give effect to congressional decrees; Congress had no authority to exact obedience, or punish disobedience, to its ordinances. This, said Hamilton in *The Federalist,* was the "great and radical vice, in the construction of the confederation . . . the principle of LEGISLATION for STATES or GOVERNMENTS, in their CORPORATE or COLLECTIVE CAPACITIES, and as contradistinguished from the INDIVIDUALS of whom they consist."

The result was that, though in theory the acts of the Confederation Congress were laws, in practice they were mere recommendations to the states. Hence, as Hamilton pointed out, the concurrence of all of the thirteen states was really needed for the effective execution of every congressional measure of importance. Such a system, Chief Justice Marshall declared in his *Life of Washington,* "could only be rescued from ignominy and contempt by finding [the states] administered by men exempt from the passions incident to human nature."

The weaknesses of the Articles of Confederation can be explained by the experience of the colonists in their struggle against parliamentary authority. The colonists were unready to concede to Congress powers which they had so strongly refused to Parliament. This was particularly true of the power to tax and the commerce power. The pre-revolutionary experience had instilled in them the belief that such powers should be exercised only by their own local assemblies.

Yet if the Articles of Confederation did less than set up that more perfect Union which Americans were soon to find necessary, the Articles' positive part in the constitutional evolution of the United States should not be overlooked. Until the Articles went into effect, the Declaration of Independence was the only written instrument binding the nation together. And, if the first central government was not as effective as later historians would have liked, its mere creation was the vital first step in the molding of the Union.

The Articles of Confederation, with all its weaknesses, did give a legal basis to the *de facto* national government which had existed under the Continental Congress. Their provision for a "perpetual Union," and the operation, however inadequate, of a government of such Union, accustomed Americans to think of themselves as one nation. Deficient though they were, the Articles, in John Marshall's characterization, "preserved the idea of Union until the good sense of the Nation adopted a more efficient system." When the Union proved defective, the question was not how to do away with it but how to make it more perfect.

Perhaps the greatest achievement of the Confederation was one not authorized by the letter of the Articles: the enactment of the Northwest Ordinance of 1787. One of the problems on which the original project of permanent Union had nearly foundered was that of resolution of the conflicting land claims of the states which asserted rights west of the Alleghenies. It was only when those states agreed to surrender their claims to Congress that the Articles of Confederation were finally ratified. To deal with these western lands, the Northwest Ordinance was passed. Applicable to the land between the Ohio and Mississippi, it provided for the eventual division of that area into not more than five nor fewer than three states, after a transitional period during which it would be governed as a territory.

The essentials of the scheme laid down in the Northwest Ordinance have governed the expansion of the United States from a federation on the Atlantic seaboard to continental extent and even, in recent years, to beyond the North American mainland. To be sure, territorial expansion is nothing new in the history of nations. Much of man's record, indeed, is nothing more than an account of the physical ebbs and flows of empire. What is novel about the American experience in this respect is the basic rejection at the beginning of the notion of conquest as determining the status of newly acquired territory. Ever since the Northwest Ordinance, the governing principle has been that no area that should come within the control of the nation should permanently be held in a territorial status. On the contrary, territory acquired by the United States, in the words of the Supreme Court over a century ago, "is acquired to become a State, and not to be held as a colony." This was the crucial accomplishment of the pre-Constitution government, which was to enable the nation to grow as a union of equal states, rather than in accordance with traditional imperial principles.

Though recent research has provided a corrective to the extreme attitude of denigration commonly expressed by historians toward the Articles of Confederation, it can scarcely be gainsaid that the government established by that instrument was inadequate for the needs of the new nation. To paraphrase Charles Warren, the Articles provided for a government without power to tax, to raise troops, to regulate commerce, or to execute or enforce its own laws and treaties—a government in which each of the states had power to tax, to make its own money, to impose its own import and export duties, and to conform or not, as it chose, to the measures enacted by the nation or the nation's requisitions for money or troops. Well might Washington declare, in 1785, that "the confederation appears to me to be little more than a shadow without the substance; and congress a nugatory body, their ordinances being little attended to."

Of particular significance in this respect was the lack of effective power to regulate commerce. "When victory relieved the Colonies from the pressure for solidarity that war had exerted," the Supreme Court tells us in a 1949 case, "a drift toward anarchy and commercial warfare between states began." Such a state of affairs naturally gave rise to serious dissensions. Real or imaginary grievances were, in Justice Joseph Story's view, multiplied in every direction; animosities and prejudices were fostered to so high a degree as to threaten at once the peace and safety of the Union. Even while the Framers sat in 1787, New Jersey passed a law taxing the lighthouse at Sandy Hook, owned by New York but situated on New Jersey land, in retaliation for New York's imposition of entrance and clearance fees for ships bound from or to New Jersey and Connecticut. Similar state laws imposing duties and commercial burdens on other states were widespread. "The oppressed and degraded state of commerce previous to the adoption of the Constitution," affirmed Chief Justice Marshall in 1827, "can scarcely be forgotten."

It has become fashionable of late to criticize Charles A. Beard's economic interpretation of the work of the Framers. At the same time, it is surely beyond question that the immediate cause of the Constitution was an economic one. "It may be doubted," Marshall tells us, "whether any of the evils proceeding from the feebleness of the Federal Government contributed more to that great revolution which introduced the present system, than the deep and general conviction that commerce ought to be regulated by Congress." It was to secure freedom of commerce—to break down the structure of interstate barriers the states were building—that the drive leading to the Convention of 1787 was initiated. The primary purpose behind Virginia's inauguration of the movement which ultimately produced the Constitution was "to take into consideration the trade of the United States; to examine the relative situations and trade of the said states; to consider how far a uniform system in their commercial regulation may be necessary to their common interest and their permanent harmony." For that purpose the Virginia legislature in January of 1786 named commissioners and proposed their meeting with those from other states. The need to federalize the regulation of commerce may thus be taken as the proximate cause of our constitutional existence down to this very day.

The resolution of the Virginia legislators and the Annapolis Convention which followed led directly to the calling of the Philadelphia Convention of 1787, which the Confederation Congress itself resolved should be appointed "for the sole purpose of revising the Articles of Confederation" and of reporting such alterations as would "render the Federal Constitution adequate to the exigencies of Government, and the preservation of the Union." The men who met in accordance with such resolve went far beyond mere amendment of the Articles and produced an entirely new charter of government and one which was to be ratified, not by Congress, but by the people themselves, in state conventions assembled for the purpose.

Until modern times the attitude of Americans toward the Framers recalled with singular fidelity that attitude with which Burke thought the Englishman of the eighteenth century should look upon the institutions of his country: "We ought to understand it according to our measure; and to venerate where we are not able to understand." Yet, if to our grandfathers and our fathers the work of the Founding Fathers was a sacred specimen of American statesmanship, in our own day the pendulum has swung somewhat the other way. Now we are told that the Constitution was less a product of farseeing sagacity than a biased attempt by the Framers to safeguard their own economic interests.

Of course, the document of 1787 reflects the economic, as well as the political, difficulties which confronted the new nation. "Most of our political evils," wrote Madison in 1786, "may be traced to our commercial ones." It was not unwonted for men of such opinion to attempt to remedy commercial evils in the instrument which they drafted. Yet the fact that the Constitution has an economic, as well as a political, basis hardly detracts from the remarkable nature of the Framers' achievement.

Such achievement would scarcely have been possible had not the Philadelphia Convention been composed of as notable an assembly as ever sat for legislative purposes—"an assembly of demi-gods," Jefferson termed them. The fifty-five men who came to Independence Hall had a background of ability and public service which admirably fitted them for the task they were undertaking. Thirty-nine of them had served in the Congress under the Articles; eight had been signers of the Declaration of Independence; eight had helped to draft their state constitutions; seven had served as chief executives of their states. Nor were these men whose productive years were all behind them. Though, as Franklin wrote, this was "*une assemblée des notables*, a convention composed of some of the principal people from the several States," more than half of them were also to become leaders in the new nation which they established: two became Presidents, one Vice-President, two Chief Justices, three Justices of the Supreme Court, and six state governors. Eighteen were elected to the first Congress under the Constitution.

Of special significance was the fact that nearly two thirds of the Framers were members of the legal profession, of whom ten had been state judges. Such training and experience in the law was essential if the document which they drafted was to prove to be a practical charter of government, rather than a mere product of academic speculation. Voltaire, in a famous exclamation, demanded the total destruction of all existing law: "Do you want good laws? Burn yours and make new ones!" Men who were themselves practitioners of the law realized better. From their own training, they knew that law was reason codified by experience. An attempt to write the fundamental law of a people on a *tabula rasa* may turn out favorably in Greek myth. In real life, the successful constitution-maker must work upon an existing political and historical mold. "Experience must be our only guide," affirmed one of the Framers. "Reason may mislead us."

Their hard-headed legal realism enabled the Founders to avoid the cardinal error that is so common among the draftsmen of fundamental laws. The men who write constitutions, all too often, seek to provide expressly for all foreseeable contingencies. Like Jeremy Bentham, they seek to be able to say: "Citizen, what is your condition? Are you a farmer? Then consult the chapter on Agriculture." The result is that most constitutions partake of all the prolixity of lengthy political codes.

The same is happily not the case with the Federal Constitution. That document, in the Supreme Court's words, "deals in general language. It did not suit the purposes of the people, in framing this great charter of our liberties, to provide for minute specifications of its powers." The great outlines are marked, the important objects designated, but the detailed particulars are left to be deduced. Only thus, the highest Court has said, could such instrument be expected "to endure through a long lapse of ages, the events of which were locked up in the inscrutable purposes of Providence."

Thomas Hardy, in describing the character of one of the women in his novels, once stated, "Like the British Constitution, she owes her success in practice to her inconsistencies in principle." There are those who would make the same assertion about the American Constitution. It is true that the Philadelphia Convention could operate effectively because the Framers were able to reconcile the important differences which existed between them. Time and again, opposing viewpoints were harmonized or recourse had to language that left open the issue. In this sense the document drafted in 1787 was, as the historian Max Farrand has said, "a bundle of compromises."

At the same time, as we survey the over-all result of its work, we must conclude that the Philadelphia Convention was dominated not so much by the spirit of compromise as by that of audacious achievement. Concessions there were, to be sure, to reconcile differences among the Framers. But these were, in the main, on subsidiary matters. In essence there was only one compromise—the Great or Connecticut Compromise—which settled the question of representation between the large and small states. Without it, there might, as a practical matter, well have been no Constitution at all.

The agreement that the states should be represented equally in the upper house, while proportional representation according to population should be the rule in the lower, may have been necessary if all the states, regardless of size, were to be able to adhere to the new Union. From the point of view of the modern constitutional historian, however, the question of legislative representation is of minor importance. The problem the compromise was designed to meet—that of conflict between the large and small states—has never since been a real one in American history.

On all the important constitutional issues before them, the Framers, in Esmond Wright's view, spoke and thought with remarkable unanimity. This was true, first of all, with regard to the crucial decision at the outset of whether there was to be a new constitution at all. The letter of their mandate limited the men of 1787 to revision of the Articles of Confederation. But, with a boldness that was to prove characteristic of all their important decisions, they determined, soon after they began their meetings, to go far beyond mere alteration of the existing document. Edmund Randolph's resolutions, unanimously adopted as the basis for the initial work of the convention, wholly ignored the Articles and provided instead for an entirely new charter of government. With the adoption of the Virginia Plan as the foundation for the Framers' work, the die was definitively cast in favor of a new constitution. When, half a month later, the New Jersey Plan was presented, its return to mere revision of the Articles was overwhelmingly rejected. As Farrand puts it, "in the course of the two weeks' discussion, many of the delegates had become accustomed to what might well have appeared to them at the outset as somewhat radical ideas."

The Philadelphia Convention resolved upon an entirely new instrument because its members were acutely aware of the essential flaws in the existing Articles. The Confederation, they knew, could not provide the effective government which the new nation needed. It is scarcely surprising that, once they had determined to make a new constitution, the Framers then devoted their major efforts at correcting the deficiencies of the Articles of Confederation. If we compare the instrument which they wrote with the Articles, we shall find that they were amazingly successful in such endeavor.

At almost the very beginning of their deliberations, the Framers resolved to eliminate what have already been termed the two fundamental defects of the government established under the Confederation. Meeting in Committee of the Whole to consider Randolph's resolutions, the convention committed itself on May 30 to the basic proposition: "That a National Government ought to be established consisting of a supreme Legislative, Executive and Judiciary." With this step the Framers went to the root of the whole matter before the convention. Under the Articles, Madison was later to explain, while the central government "operated within the extent of its authority through requisitions on the Confederated States, and rested on the sanction of State Legislatures, the Government to take its place was to operate within the extent of its powers directly and coercively on individuals, and to receive the higher sanction of the people of the States."

The Confederation, we saw, rested the authority of the nation upon the states, not on the people. And there was no coercive authority provided for its decrees. In Charles Warren's characterization, Congress could only supplicate; it could not enforce. The Constitution rests directly on the people, as its Preamble and mode of ratification specifically indicate. And, more important, the measures of the Federal Government are vested with compulsive effect. They operate directly on individuals and do not require state implementation before they can be rendered effective. The government of the nation was, as George Mason said, to be one which would "directly operate on individuals and possess compulsive power on the people of the United States."

The device adopted by the Framers to attain this result was as simple as it was effective. The key constitutional provision in this respect is the supremacy clause of Article VI. Under it, not only the Constitution, but all federal laws and treaties are expressly declared to be "the supreme Law of the Land." Nor is the principle of federal supremacy thus enunciated only a hortatory one. On the contrary, under the supremacy clause, "the Judges in every State shall be bound" by federal laws and treaties, "anything in the Constitution or Laws of any State to the Contrary notwithstanding."

The acts of the Federal Government, in other words, are to be operative as supreme law throughout the Union. They possess such status because they are self-executing in that they prescribe rules that, standing alone, are enforceable in all the courts of the land. This enables the mandates of Washington to prevail without any need for state implementation. "The states," declared Chief Justice Marshall in *McCulloch v. Maryland,* "have no power . . . to retard, impede, burden, or in any manner control, the operations of the constitutional laws enacted by congress to carry into execution the powers vested in the general government. This is we think, the unavoidable consequence of that supremacy which the constitution has declared."

Through the supremacy clause, the Framers prevented the Federal Government from becoming subordinate to the states in the manner that had destroyed the effectiveness of the original Confederation. In addition, they provided that the government of the nation was to be a fully developed structure, with separate legislative, executive, and judicial branches. That they would so provide was clear from almost the beginning of their deliberations, for Randolph's resolution, already quoted, contemplated a national government divided into three distinct departments. "The moment, indeed," wrote Madison in 1835, "a real Constitution was looked for as a substitute for the Confederacy, the distribution of the Government into the usual departments became a matter of course with all who speculated on the prospective changes."

What the Framers provided for, in establishing a tripartite central government whose decrees are directly operative as law on the people of the nation, was the existence throughout the United States of two centers of government, each with its own complete apparatus of lawmaking and law enforcement. Two governments, provided with the complete accouterments of political power, coexist and issue their mandates, binding directly their respective citizens. Neither is dependent upon the other for the execution of its ordinances. Instead, in James Bryce's description, there are two governments covering the same ground, yet distinct and separate in their action.

We have by now become so accustomed to the federal system established by the Constitution that we have tended to forget that its creation in 1787 was a political invention of the highest order. The United States, to be sure, was not the first example of a federated body politic. In prior federations, however, as under the Articles of 1781, the member states had generally agreed to obey the mandates of a common government for certain stipulated purposes, but had retained to themselves the right of ordaining and enforcing the laws of the Confederation. The form of federation offered by the Framers was new in history. "I know not," said a member of New York's ratifying convention, "that history furnishes an example of a confederated Republic coercing the States composing it, by the mild influence of laws operating on the individuals of those states. This, therefore, I suppose to be a new experiment in politics." Well could de

Tocqueville assert that the federal frame established at Philadelphia should "be considered a great discovery in modern political science."

To make the federal system work, it was essential that the central government be more than a mere paper polity. More specifically, it had to be given the vital substantive powers whose lack had rendered the Confederation sterile. What those powers are was stated in classic language by Chief Justice Marshall: "the great powers to lay and collect taxes; to borrow money; to regulate commerce; to declare and conduct a war; and to raise and support armies and navies. The sword and the purse, all the external relations, and no inconsiderable portion of the industry of the nation." These are precisely the powers vested in the Federal Government by the Constitution—powers which have enabled it to fulfill the great purposes intended by the Framers.

Of particular significance is the express grant of the power to tax and the power to regulate commerce. The former freed the nation completely from the financial dependence on the states which had, in the phrase of a 1786 congressional committee, hazarded the very existence of the Union. The latter enabled the Federal Government to put an end to the economic autarchy of the states. More than that, the commerce clause of Article I, section 8, has promoted a system of free trade throughout the Union. "Our system," the highest Court declared in 1949, "is that every farmer and every craftsman shall be encouraged to produce by the certainty that he will have free access to every market in the Nation. . . . Such was the vision of the Founders." Upon such vision has been based the commercial success of the nation. To cite Felix Frankfurter "With all doubts as to what history teaches, few seem clearer than the beneficial consequences which have flowed from this conception of the Commerce Clause."

It has already been mentioned that the Framers were virtually unanimous in their decision to base the constitutional framework which they were creating upon the separation of powers. The administrative ineptitude of the Congress, in whom all the powers granted by the Confederation were vested, made the division of the new government into three autonomous departments—each endowed with the powers appropriate to it—a practical, as well as a philosophical, necessity.

By setting up the Federal Government with distinct executive and judicial branches, completely separate from the legislative department, the Founders were able to insure that each of the three great powers essential to a true national government would be effectively exercised. This was particularly true with regard to the establishment of an independent executive department. The composition of such a department posed a very real dilemma. On the one hand, there was the pressing need for an Executive strong enough to penetrate to the remotest reaches of the Union. At the same time, there was the danger of stirring up the prevalent popular fear of monarchy. Those hostile to the Union they were creating, the men of 1787 well knew, would be all too ready to picture the new Executive with a diadem on his brow and the purple flowing in his train.

That the Framers resolved the problem by the creation of the Presidency was an act of political boldness of the first magnitude. By rejecting the notion of a plural Executive, the unity essential to effective action was provided for. By discarding the idea of election by the legislature, the independence necessary for presidential power and prestige was established. "The Executives of the States," complained Madison, "are in general little more than cyphers, the Legislatures omnipotent." The same could scarcely be said of the polity provided for by the able gentlemen who burned midnight candles in Philadelphia the better part of two centuries ago.

Scarcely less significant, from a constitutional point of view, was the provision of an independent judiciary as one of the three co-ordinate departments. The want of a judiciary power, asserts Hamilton in *The Federalist,* crowned the defects of the Articles of Confederation. National laws must remain ineffective without national courts to expound and define their meaning and operation. Without an independent judicial department—with the authority to ascertain and enforce the powers of the Union—the laws, the treaties, and even the Constitution of the United States would become a dead letter. By setting up a federal judicial branch, the Framers gave to every person having a claim involving a federal question a right to submit his case to a court of the nation. The judicial arm of the nation itself is given the controlling word in the enforcement of its basic instrument and laws.

The Framers crowned the positive powers of the new government by deriving them, not from the states, but from the people. Next to the determination that there was to be a new constitution, not a mere revision of the existing Articles, this was perhaps the most daring of all the decisions made at the Philadelphia Convention. For it meant that the Constitution was the act of the people themselves, not that of the states which had joined together to form the Confederation.

Speaking in the Virginia Convention in 1788, Patrick Henry demanded to know "what right had they to say, *We, the people?* Who authorized them to speak the language of, *We, the people,* instead of, *We, the States?*" In strict law, Henry may have been correct; the Framers sat under the resolution of the Confederation Congress which gave them only limited authority to revise the Articles and then report any such alterations to Congress and the state legislatures, which revisions would become effective only "when agreed to in Congress, and confirmed by the States." But the limits of their original mandate had been completely overturned by the seminal decision to write a new governmental charter. In acting on that decision, it was not unwonted for the writers of the document to consider themselves more than mere agents of Congress or the states. The draftsmen wrote in the name of the people of the nation and they provided for ratification by the people, in conventions assembled, entirely omitting any reference to the Confederation Congress in the Ratification Article.

The Framers were well aware of the legal significance of their action in the name of "We the People." During the debate on the method of ratification, Madison stated that he "considered the difference between a system founded on the Legislatures only, and one founded on the people, to be the true difference between a *league* or *treaty,* and a *Constitution.*" From this it follows emphatically that the document drawn up in 1787 is not a mere compact between the states. "This is not a government founded upon a compact," declared James Wilson in the 1788 Pennsylvania ratification convention. "It is founded upon the power of the people."

The Constitution itself is plainly inconsistent with the notion of sovereignty of the states. Though the Union, like all federations, is composed of a number of autonomous political entities, the Constitution did not emanate from them as independent commonwealths. The Preamble itself bears witness to the fact that the Constitution was the act not of the states but of the nation. It sets up, in Marshall's celebrated language, "emphatically, and truly, a government of the people. In form and in substance it emanates from them." The states make up, but they did not make, the Union.

In considering the work of the Framers, we have until now stressed the Constitution as a positive charter vesting the nation with an effective political structure endowed with the affirmative authority needed to meet the manifold problems of government. It would, however, be erroneous to consider the Constitution only as a grant of governmental power. Just as important is its function as a limitation upon such power. Having just engaged in a revolution against what they conceived to be excessive governmental authority, one may doubt that the Framers were creating their new polity in the British image. Instead, the document which they wrote was one under which governmental powers were both conferred and circumscribed. The Constitution, despite Macaulay's noted assertion, is emphatically not meant to be "all sail and no anchor."

The restrictions imposed by the Framers are of two types. In the first place, there is the very structure of the new government, with its consistent emphasis upon the division of governmental power. By such consistent division, the Framers sought to insure against the type of government which they felt had brought on the Revolution. "The doctrine of the separation of powers," Louis D. Brandeis has stated, "was adopted by the Convention of 1787 not to promote efficiency but to preclude the exercise of arbitrary power. The purpose was not to avoid friction, but, by means of the inevitable friction incident to the distribution of the governmental powers among three departments, to save the people from autocracy."

In addition, significant express restrictions were imposed upon the new governmental authority, both in the original Constitution and in the first ten amendments, whose adoption was generally considered as the condition for ratification. These restrictions are the essential safeguards for the rights of the individual. In Madison's words, they contain "effective provisions against the encroachment on particular rights and those safeguards which they have been long accustomed to have interposed between them and the magistrate who exercises the sovereign power."

Even more important perhaps than the specific restrictions contained in the document drawn up in 1787 was the basic limitation upon governmental power imposed by the very concept of a written constitution itself. Here precisely was the great contribution of the Framers to the science of government: the notion of a written fundamental law which limits the powers of the people and their political delegates.

This idea was not, to be sure, novel with the Framers; it was instead the fruit of both the colonial and the revolutionary experience. But it was the men of 1787 who made the most significant translation of it into practical reality. It was they who brought to culmination the idea of a written document vested with positive effect as the supreme law of the land, and serving, as such, as a basic check upon the will of the governors at any given time. By such a document, they classified certain things as organic fundamentals, which could not be changed except by the cumbersome process of amendment. Because of their work, the Supreme Court could later say, "It is the peculiar value of a written constitution that it places in unchanging form limitations upon legislative action, and thus gives a permanence and stability to popular government which would otherwise be lacking."

The instrument drafted in Philadelphia remains the fundamentally permanent feature in a system which has undergone so many transformations since it was instituted in an age of knee breeches and three-cornered hats. Amid all the crises of government, social and economic exigencies, even the all-consuming demands of total conflict—the Constitution has stood as the one basic constant in an inherently inconstant world. As it was put at the outset, by William Paterson, a member of the highest bench, "Notwithstanding the competition of opposing interests, and the violence of contending parties, it remains firm and immovable, as a mountain amidst the strife of storms, or a rock in the ocean amidst the raging of the waves."

III

COLOSSUS

ON THE north and south walls of the Supreme Court Chamber in Washington are carved two marble panels depicting processions of historical lawgivers. Of the eighteen figures on the panels, only the last one is famous as a judge, and he is the one American represented: John Marshall. This is more than mere coincidence; it sharply illustrates a basic difference between American law and that in other countries.

The great lawgivers in other systems have been mighty monarchs, of the type of Hammurabi and Justinian, divinely inspired prophets like Moses, philosophers such as Confucius, or scholars like Hugo Grotius or Blackstone. We in the United States have certainly had our share of the last two types of lawgiver—particularly among the men who drew up organic documents during and after the Revolution. Yet it is not a Jefferson or a Madison who is depicted as *the* American lawgiver, but the great Chief Justice who, in Benjamin N. Cardozo's characterization, gave to the Constitution the impress of his own mind. It was Marshall who established the role of the Supreme Court as the authoritative expounder of the Constitution, and it was he who exercised this role to lay the legal foundations of a strong nation, endowed with all the authority needed to enable it to govern effectively.

To be sure, the constitutional history of the new Republic does not start with Marshall. The Constitution had been in operation for over a decade before he took his place on the highest bench. Nor can it be denied that those first years of the new Union were pregnant ones from a constitutional point of view. This was particularly true so far as the working of the executive branch was concerned. The Framers had written Article II with purposed vagueness, knowing that excessive detail would only hamper that department's ability to meet unforeseen circumstances. The structure of the Presidency and its actual operation have depended as much upon unwritten executive practice as the letter of the basic written document.

During its first decade, "The executive Power" established by the Constitution received much of its detailed form and content. It was established at the very beginning that the President should possess the power to remove the heads of the executive departments. He was freed from direct dependence upon the Senate in the performance of his duties by Washington's rejection of the notion of the upper house as a council of state, which some of the Framers had entertained. Senatorial power to "advise and consent" thus became a mere veto power over appointments and treaties. In the place of the Senate, the Cabinet developed as an advisory body to the President. And, in some ways most important, Presidential primacy was established in the field of foreign affairs. The Jay Treaty and Washington's 1793 Proclamation of Neutrality both demonstrated the extent of presidential power in that field. If the Framers intended to divide foreign affairs between the President and the Congress, Washington's actions early settled that, in practice, the lion's share went to the former.

"The judicial Power" established by Article III was also given specific structural form during the first ten years of the new Republic. The Judiciary Act of 1789 laid down the basic organization of the federal judicial department—with courts of general jurisdiction, as well as intermediate appellate courts, located throughout the country and a Supreme Court as ultimate appellate tribunal. A right of appeal to the highest Court from the state courts in cases involving federal questions was provided for.

To understand the contribution of Marshall, however, one must look at the new judicial department, not through twentieth-century spectacles, but through the eyes of men living a decade after the Constitution went into effect. "The judiciary," wrote Hamilton in *The Federalist,* "is beyond comparison the weakest of the three departments of power." This remark was amply justified by the situation of the fledgling judiciary before Marshall's time.

It is hard for us today to realize that, at the beginning at least, a seat on the supreme bench was anything but the culmination of a legal career that it has since become. John Jay, the first Chief Justice, resigned to become Governor of New York (certainly a lesser position by present-day standards) and Alexander Hamilton declined Jay's post, being, in the words of the Supreme Court historian, "anxious to renew his law practice and political activities in New York." Robert Harrison declined a place on the first Supreme Court (after having been confirmed by the Senate) to become chancellor of Maryland. The weakness of the early Supreme Court is forcibly demonstrated by the fact that, in the building of the new Capitol, that tribunal was completely overlooked and no chamber provided for it. Thus, as Marshall's biographer, Albert Beveridge, points out, when the seat of government was moved to Washington, the high bench crept into an undignified chamber in the basement beneath the Senate Chamber.

Such was the low prestige of the Supreme Court when John Marshall was appointed to its central chair in 1801. All this was to change during his tenure of the highest judicial office. By the force of his character and the soundness of his legal judgment, he was to transform the supreme tribunal into the head of a fully co-ordinate department, endowed with the ultimate authority of safeguarding the ark of the Constitution. More than that, he was to weave the legal fabric of Union in such a way that, as Charles Wiltse puts it, he transmuted the federal structure created by the Founders into a nation strong enough to withstand even the shock of civil war.

All history, says Emerson, is subjective; in other words there is properly no history, only biography. As a wholesale generalization, this may be debatable. But it is surely true of the early constitutional history of the United States, which can be stated essentially in terms of Marshall's contribution. Yet, if we look to the background of the man himself, he certainly seemed ill equipped for the formidable task to which he was ultimately called. One who reads the modest account of his early life in his famous autobiographical letter to Joseph Story is bound to be amazed at the meagerness of his education and training, both generally and in the law itself. His only formal schooling consisted of a year under the tuition of a clergyman, as well as another under a tutor who resided with his family. For the rest, his learning was under the superintendence of his father, who, Marshall himself concedes, "had received a very limited education."

His study for the bar was equally rudimentary. During the winter of 1779–1780, while on leave from the Army, "I availed myself of this inactive interval for attending a course of law lectures given by Mr. Wythe, and of lectures of Natural philosophy given by Mr. Madison then President of William and Mary College." He attended law lectures for only six weeks—a time so short, according to Beveridge, that, in the opinion of the students, "those who finish this study [law] in a few months, either have strong natural parts or else they know little about it." We may doubt, indeed, whether Marshall was prepared even to take full advantage of so short a law course. He had just fallen in love with his wife-to-be, and his notebook (which is preserved) indicates that his thoughts were at least as much upon his sweetheart as upon the lecturer's wisdom.

Shakespeare, according to Alfred North Whitehead, wrote better poetry for not knowing too much. It may appear paradoxical to make the same assertion with regard to the greatest of American judges, for judicial ability normally depends, in large measure, upon depth of legal learning. It must, however, be emphasized that Marshall's was not the ordinary judicial role. Great judges are typically not radical innovators. "I venture to suggest," states Justice Frankfurter, "that had they the mind of such originators, the bench is not the place for its employment. Transforming thought implies too great a break with the past, implies too much discontinuity, to be imposed upon society by one who is entrusted with enforcing its law."

Marshall's role, on the other hand, was as much that of legislator as judge. His was the task of translating the constitutional framework into the reality of decided cases. As one commentator puts it, "he hit the Constitution much as the Lord hit the chaos, at a time when everything needed creating." The need was for formative genius—for the transfiguring thought that the judge normally is not called upon to impose on society. Had Marshall been more learned in the law, he might not have performed his creative task as well as he did. Had he, in Andrew McLaughlin's characterization, been more the trained lawyer, thoroughly steeped in technical learning and entangled in the intricacies of the law, he might not have been so great a judge; for his role called for the talent and the insight of a statesman capable of looking beyond the confines of strict law to the needs of a vigorous nation entered upon the task of occupying a continent.

One aspect of Marshall's education should not be overlooked, though it was far removed from the traditional type of schooling. This was his service as a soldier of the Revolution. It was, his biographer informs us, his military experience—on the march, in camp, and on the battlefield—that taught Marshall the primary lesson of the necessity of strong efficient government: "Valley Forge was a better training for Marshall's peculiar abilities than Oxford or Cambridge could have been." Above all, his service with Washington confirmed in him the overriding loyalty to an effective union. Love of the Union and the maxim "United we stand, divided we fall," he once wrote, were "imbibed . . . so thoroughly that they constituted a part of my being. I carried them with me into the army . . . in a common cause believed by all to be most precious, and where I was confirmed in the habit of considering America as my country and Congress as my government." In his most powerful opinions, it has been well said, Marshall appears to us to be talking, not in the terms of technical law, but as one of Washington's soldiers who had suffered that the nation might live.

When all is said and done, nevertheless, an element of wonder remains when we contemplate Marshall's work. The magisterial character of his opinions, marching with measured cadence to their inevitable logical conclusion, has never been equaled, much less surpassed, in judicial history. Clarity, conciseness, eloquence

—these are the Marshall hallmarks, which made his opinions irresistible, combined as they were with what Edward S. Corwin has termed his "tiger instinct for the jugular vein," his rigorous pursuit of logical consequences, his power of stating a case, his scorn of qualifying language, the pith and balance of his phrasing, and the developing momentum of his argument. His is the rare legal document whose words can be read and meaning understood by the layman as well as the learned practitioner. And all this from a man almost without formal schooling, either in literature or the law. Were we not historically certain of the fact, we might have as much doubt that such an individual, possessed as he was only of raw genius plus the courage to use it, really wrote the masterful opinions that served as the doctrinal foundation of a great nation as some have expressed with regard to the authorship by an unschooled Elizabethan actor of the supreme literary products of the English language.

It is customary to designate a particular Supreme Court by the name of its Chief. Such designation was more than mere formalism when Marshall presided over the highest bench. From the time when he first took his place in its central chair to his death thirty-four years later, it was emphatically the Marshall Court that stood at the head of the federal judicial system. A Chief Justice, we are told, must get his real eminence, not from his office, but from the qualities he brings to it. He must possess the elusive quality of leadership. That quality Marshall possessed in outstanding degree. He dominated his Court as has no other Chief Justice. If the work of the supreme bench, as Justice Frankfurter tells us, is an orchestral rather than a solo performance, still Marshall's manner of presiding over his Court may be likened to Toscanini's manner of presiding over an orchestra—with the added feature of the leader almost always appearing as the principal soloist as well.

Throughout his judicial career, Marshall's consistent aim was to use the Supreme Court to lay the constitutional foundation of an effective nation. Before such an aim could be realized, the prestige and power of the high tribunal itself had to be increased. For the bench to which Marshall was first appointed could hardly hope to play the positive role in welding the new nation that the great Chief Justice conceived.

As soon as Marshall began to discharge his duties as head of the highest Court, Beveridge's classic life of the great Chief Justice informs us, "he quietly began to strengthen the Supreme Court. He did this by one of those acts of audacity that later marked the assumptions of power which rendered his career historic. For the first time the Chief Justice disregarded the custom of the delivery of opinions by the Justices *seriatim,* and, instead, calmly assumed the function of announcing, himself, the views of that tribunal. Thus Marshall took the first step in impressing the country with the unity of the highest court of the Nation."

Before Marshall, the Supreme Court followed the English practice of having opinions pronounced by each of the individual Justices. The practice of having instead one opinion of the Court was begun by Marshall in the very first case decided after he became Chief Justice. The change from a number of individual opinions to the Court opinion was admirably suited to strengthen the prestige of the fledgling Supreme Court. To John Marshall, the needed authority and dignity of the Court could be attained only if the principles it proclaimed were pronounced by a united tribunal. To win conclusiveness and fixity for its constructions, he strove for a Court with a single voice. How well he succeeded in this is shown by the reception accorded Justice William Johnson, when the latter sought for the first time to express his own views, in a case where he disagreed with the decision of the Court. "During the rest of the Session," he plaintively affirmed in a letter to Thomas Jefferson, "I heard nothing but Lectures on the Indecency of Judges cutting at each other, and the Loss of Reputation which the Virginia appellate Court had sustained by pursuing such a course."

Yet, though constitutional decisions have thus, since Marshall's innovation, been the offspring of the highest Court as a whole, it is important to bear in mind that their expression is individual. As Justice Frankfurter has said, "The voice of the Court cannot avoid imparting to its opinions the distinction of its own accent. Marshall spoke for the Court. But *he* spoke." And this enabled him to formulate in his own way the landmarks of our constitutional law.

Marshall's first concern, after his appointment to the high bench, was to assert for the judicial department the powers needed to enable it to forge the constitutional bonds of a strong nation. The essential step in that direction was taken only two years after he became Chief Justice, with the reading in 1803 of the opinion in the great case of *Marbury v. Madison.*

That case is now rightly considered as the very keystone of the American constitutional arch, for, in it, the Supreme Court first ruled that it possessed the authority to review the constitutionality of acts of the legislative department. Yet, when the case came before the high bench, it seemed to present anything but the question of judicial review. Marbury, who had been appointed to be a justice of the peace in the District of Columbia by President Adams at the very end of his Administration, had been confirmed by the Senate; his commission had been signed and sealed, but had not yet been delivered when Jefferson took office. The new President ordered Madison, just designated as Secretary of State, to withhold the commission. Marbury then applied directly to the Supreme Court for a writ of mandamus ordering the Secretary to deliver the commission. He did so under section 13 of the Judiciary Act of 1789, which vested the highest Court with original jurisdiction to issue mandamus against federal officials.

In form, all that *Marbury v. Madison* appeared to present was the question of whether mandamus could issue in such a case against the Secretary of State. In answering it, the Supreme Court could apparently either disavow its power over the executive branch and dismiss the application, or it could assert such power and order the commission to be delivered. To choose the first course would have been to abdicate the essentials of "The judicial Power" conferred by the Constitution. But the second was no more satisfactory. For, while it would declare the vindication of authority to hold the Executive to the law, such declaration would, without a doubt, remain a mere paper one. There was no way for the Court to enforce its mandate against the Administration. In fact, bearing in mind the low esteem in which the high bench was still held, it is doubtful that it could have emerged other than fatally wounded from a direct clash with the Executive. Hence, as Marshall's biographer puts it, no matter which horn of the dilemma Marshall selected, it was hard to see how his views could escape impalement.

That Marshall was able to choose neither is perhaps the best tribute of all to his judicial statesmanship. He escaped from the dilemma by convincing his brethren on the Court of the unconstitutionality of section 13 of the Judiciary Act on the ground that, since the original jurisdiction conferred upon the Supreme Court by the Constitution was exclusive, it could not validly be enlarged by statute. Thus the Court could deny Marbury's application, not because the executive branch was above the law (Marshall's opinion, on the contrary, contains a strong repudiation of that claim), but because the Court itself did not possess the original jurisdiction to issue the writ requested.

To reach the result just stated, to be sure, the high bench had to rule that the statute conferring such competence was invalid and, in so doing, assert the judicial power to review the constitutionality of acts of Congress. From a strategic point of view, at the same time, a better case could not have been chosen for declaration of the power which has ever since been considered the palladium of the constitutional structure. Since the Court's decision denied relief, there was nothing to execute—nothing which would give rise to direct conflict with the Administration. More than that, the assertion of the greatest of all judicial powers was made in a case which ostensibly denied authority to the Court. It is in this sense that Marshall's opinion in *Marbury v. Madison* deserves its characterization by Corwin as a political coup of the first magnitude. The Jeffersonians themselves found it hard to attack a decision which declined, even from the hands of the Congress, jurisdiction to which the highest Court was not entitled by the Constitution.

From a historical point of view, *Marbury v. Madison* is of crucial importance as the first case establishing the power of the Supreme Court to review constitutionality. And it was of cardinal significance that that vital power be firmly established at the outset, in terms so firm and clear that its existence has never since been legally doubted. Had Marshall not confirmed the review power over legislative acts in his magisterial manner, it is entirely possible that it would never have been insisted upon. For it was not until the *Dred Scott* case in 1857 that the authority to invalidate a federal statute was next exercised by the Supreme Court. Had Marshall not taken his stand in *Marbury v. Madison,* nearly sixty years would have passed without any question arising as to the omnipotence of Congress. After so long a period of judicial acquiescence in congressional supremacy, as Beveridge points out, it is probable that opposition to it would have been futile.

Countless commentators have pointed out the lack of originality in Marshall's holding that the judges possessed the review power. To one familiar with the fact that law, like the history of which Frederic W. Maitland speaks, is a seamless web, such a revelation with regard to Marshall's contribution states but an inevitable truism. Of course, the law laid down by Marshall was inextricably woven with that expounded by his contemporaries and predecessors. Judicial review, as an essential element of the law, was part of the legal tradition of the time, derived from both the colonial and revolutionary experience. With the appearance during the Revolution of written constitutions, the review power began to be stated in modern terms. Between the Revolution and *Marbury v. Madison,* state courts asserted or exercised the power in at least twenty cases. Marshall himself could affirm, in *Marbury v. Madison,* not that the Constitution establishes judicial review, but only that it "confirms and strengthens the principle." Soon after the Constitution went into effect, assertions of review authority were made by a number of federal judges.

That Marshall's opinion was not radical innovation does not at all detract from its importance. The great Chief Justice, like Jefferson in writing the Declaration of Independence, may have merely set down in clear form what had already been previously declared. Yet, as Marshall's biographer observes, Thomas Jefferson and John Marshall as private citizens in Charlottesville and Richmond might have written Declarations and Opinions all their lives, and today none but the curious student would know that such men had ever lived. It was the authoritative position which those two great Americans happened to occupy that has given immortality to their enunciations. If Marshall's achievement in *Marbury v. Madison* was not transformation but only articulation, what has made it momentous is the fact that it was magisterial articulation as positive law by the highest judicial officer of the land.

Political theorists have doubted whether the assumption by Marshall and his colleagues of the review power was justified by the Constitution or was only an act of judicial usurpation. One concerned with the constitutional history of the Republic can have no such doubts. *Marbury v. Madison* authoritatively settled the review power of the judges in a manner that has never since been questioned, at least so far as our constitutional law has been concerned.

To one trained in the law, the power to decide on constitutionality is the very essence of judicial power. The authority to declare constitutionality flows naturally from the judicial duty to determine the law. *Marbury v. Madison* declares:

> It is emphatically the province and duty of the judicial department to say what the law is. Those who apply the rule to particular cases, must of necessity expound and interpret that rule. If two laws conflict with each other, the courts must decide on the operation of each. So if a law be in opposition to the constitution; if both the law and the constitution apply to a particular case, so that the court must either decide that case conformably to the law, disregarding the constitution; or conformably to the constitution, disregarding the law; the court must determine which of these conflicting rules governs the case. This is of the very essence of judicial duty.

One may go further and say that judicial review, as first declared in *Marbury v. Madison,* has become the *sine qua non* of our constitutional machinery: draw out this particular bolt, and the machinery falls to pieces.

Addressing the court in the *Five Knights' Case* (one of the great state trials of Stuart England), the Attorney General, arguing for the Crown, asked, "Shall any say, The King cannot do this? No, we may only say, He will not do this." It was precisely to insure that in the American system one would be able to say,

"The State *cannot* do this," that the people enacted a written constitution containing basic limitations upon the powers of government. Of what avail would such limitations be, however, if there were no legal machinery to enforce them? An organic instrument is naught but empty words if it cannot be enforced by the courts. It is judicial review that makes the provisions of a constitution more than mere maxims of political morality.

To hold as Marshall did in *Marbury v. Madison* that the Supreme Court could review the constitutionality of acts of Congress is, however, to lay down only half of the doctrine of judicial review. According to a noted statement by Justice Holmes, indeed, it is the less important half. "I do not think," he asserted, "the United States would come to an end if we lost our power to declare an Act of Congress void. I do think the Union would be imperilled if we could not make that declaration as to the laws of the several states." The power to pass on the validity of state legislation is a necessary part of the review power if the Constitution is truly to be maintained as supreme law throughout the Union.

It was in the 1810 case of *Fletcher v. Peck* that the Supreme Court first exercised the power to hold a state law unconstitutional. In ruling that a Georgia statute violated the contract clause of Article I, section 10, of the Federal Constitution, Marshall, who delivered the opinion, declared categorically that the state of Georgia could not be viewed as a single, unconnected sovereign power, on whom no other restrictions are imposed than those found in her own constitution. On the contrary, she is a member of the Union, "and that Union has a constitution the supremacy of which all acknowledge, and which imposes limits to the legislatures of the several states, which none claim a right to pass."

In *Fletcher v. Peck,* Marshall, in Beveridge's description, laid the second stone in the structure of American constitutional law. Yet even this was still not enough to enable the Supreme Court to maintain the Constitution as the supreme law of the land. In addition to the power to review the validity of legislative acts of both the nation and the states, review power over the judgments of the state courts is also necessary. In a system in which state judicatures coexist with those of the nation, vested with equal competence to pronounce judgment on constitutional issues, it is essential that their judgments of such issues be subjected to the overriding control of the highest tribunal. The review power over state courts in such cases is necessary if the high bench is to uphold national supremacy when it conflicts with state law or is challenged by state authority.

The appellate power of the Supreme Court over state court decisions, in order to harmonize them with the Constitution, laws, and treaties of the United States, was established in two memorable decisions by the Marshall Court. The first of them was rendered in 1816 in *Martin v. Hunter's Lessee.* That case arose out of the refusal of the highest court of Virginia to obey the mandate issued by the Supreme Court in an earlier case in which the Virginia court's decision had been reversed on the ground that it was contrary to a treaty of the United States. The Virginia judges had asserted that they were not subject to the highest bench's appellate power "under a sound construction of the constitution of the United States" and ruled that the provision of the first Judiciary Act which "extends the appellate jurisdiction of the Supreme Court to this court, is not in pursuance of the constitution of the United States."

The Supreme Court, in an opinion by Justice Story, categorically rejected the holding that it could not be vested with appellate jurisdiction over state court decisions. Marshall himself did not deliver the opinion because a personal interest in the case led him to decline to participate. There is no doubt, however, that Story's opinion was strongly influenced by the Marshall view on judicial power. Beveridge tells us, indeed, that it was commonly supposed that Marshall "practically dictated" Story's opinion. Be that as it may, the opinion was certainly one that, save for some turgidity of language, the great Chief Justice could have written.

Five years later, in the case of *Cohens v. Virginia,* Marshall himself was given the opportunity to demonstrate that such was the case. Defendants there had been convicted in a Virginia court of violating that state's law prohibiting the sale of lottery tickets. They sought a writ of error from the Supreme Court on the ground that, since the lottery in question had been authorized by an act of Congress, the state prohibitory law was invalid since it conflicted with federal law. Again it was claimed that the highest tribunal had no appellate power over the state courts. With typical force, Marshall declared that such an argument was itself contrary to the Constitution. The states, he affirmed, are not independent sovereignties; they are members of one great nation—a nation endowed by the basic document with a government competent to attain all national objects.

In a polity based upon the principle of national supremacy, it is consistent with sound reason to make all the departments of the nation supreme, in respect to those objects of vital national interest and insofar as is necessary to their attainment. "The exercise of the appellate power over those judgments of the state tribunals which may contravene the constitution or laws of the United States, is, we believe, essential to the attainment of those objects." Let the nature and objects of the Union be considered, let the great principles on which the constitutional framework rests be examined, and the result must be that the Court of the nation must be given the power of revising the decisions of local tribunals on questions which affect the nation.

According to Marshall's biographer, the opinion in *Cohens v. Virginia* is "one of the strongest and most enduring strands of that mighty cable woven by him to hold the American people together as a united and imperishable nation." Certain it is that Marshall's masterful opinion conclusively settled the competence of the high bench to review the decisions of state courts. Since *Cohens v. Virginia,* state attempts to make themselves the final arbiters in cases involving the Constitution, laws, and treaties of the United States have been foredoomed to defeat before the bar of the highest tribunal.

With the decision in *Cohens v. Virginia,* the structure of judicial power erected by the Marshall Court was completed. The authority of the judicial department to enforce the Constitution against both the national and state governments became an accepted part of American constitutional law. All governmental acts, whether of the nation or the states, now had to run the gantlet of review by the highest bench to determine whether they were constitutional. And that Court itself was now the veritable supreme tribunal of the land, for it was vested with the last word over the state, as well as the federal, judiciaries.

The Marshall Court did not obtain this august position without opposition, often violent, within both the national and state governments. In particular, the work of Marshall in strengthening the judicial department was strongly resisted by the Jeffersonian party which was dominant in the other two departments. Jefferson was, indeed, Marshall's principal antagonist throughout his life. To the great democrat, control of the validity of governmental acts by nonelected judges "would place us under the despotism of an oligarchy." He never really appreciated the need for judicial review as the true safeguard of constitutional rights against the power of government.

The Jeffersonians did not confine their opposition to the judges to verbal criticism. Instead, they sought to use the weapon of impeachment to bend the judicial department to their will. Their efforts in that direction culminated in the 1805 attempt to secure the removal by impeachment of Justice Samuel Chase, then a member of the highest Court. The charges against Chase were based on his acts while on the bench and were far removed from the "high Crimes and Misdemeanors" required by the Constitution. Rather, it was generally recognized that the impeachment was political in purpose. As Senator William Branch Giles, the Jeffersonian leader in the upper house, candidly expressed it to John Quincy Adams while the Chase trial was pending, "We want your offices, for the purpose of giving them to men who will fill them better." It was widely believed that the Chase impeachment was to be but the first step in the Jeffersonian plan. "I perceive," wrote John Quincy Adams, "that the impeachment system is to be pursued, and the whole bench of the Supreme Court to be swept away, because their offices are wanted."

The arrangements for the Chase trial, we are informed, were as dramatic as the event itself. The pomp of the Warren Hastings impeachment, when, says Lord Macaulay, "The grey old walls were hung with scarlet," was still vivid in the minds of all, and perhaps in imitation, the Senate Chamber was also "fitted up in a style of appropriate elegance. . . . Benches, covered with crimson." The trial itself resulted in an acquittal, for enough senators of the Jeffersonian party were convinced by the argument of the defense: "Our property, our liberty, our lives can only be protected by independent judges" to make the vote for conviction fall short of the constitutional majority.

The failure of the Chase impeachment was a capital event in the constitutional development of the nation. Had Chase been removed, it would have made impossible the independence of the judiciary upon which our organic structure rests. The Chase acquittal, as a matter of history, put an end to the danger of judicial removal on political grounds. "The Senate's verdict of 'Not Guilty,' " Chief Justice Arthur T. Vanderbilt says, "put an end to a theory of judicial tenure that would have meant the annihilation of an independent judiciary." Since 1805, though impeachment proceedings have been brought against nine other federal judges, in none of these cases was the effort to secure removal based upon political reasons.

The Chase acquittal meant that the Marshall Court could exercise the constitutional authority asserted by it without fear or favor. Judicial power, it should not be forgotten, was to Marshall not an end in itself, but only a means to attain the end of a sound national structure. Once he had obtained for the high Court the authority to enforce the Constitution, and once the independence had been secured that is the essential prerequisite for the fearless exercise of such authority, Marshall could turn the judicial instrument to the forging of the legal bonds of a strong Union. The nationalism nurtured at Valley Forge was to flower in the great decisions delivered at the height of his career by which were hewn the highroad of the nation's destiny.

Of Marshall's decisions employing judicial power to lay down the doctrinal foundations of an effective nation, two are of the greatest consequence: *McCulloch v. Maryland* and *Gibbons v. Ogden.* The first established principles essential to the very existence of the Federal Government; the second rendered effective the nation's most important substantive peacetime power.

Of the 1819 case of *McCulloch v. Maryland,* Marshall's biographer wrote that the opinion there "has so decisively influenced the growth of the Nation that, by many, it is considered as only second in importance to the Constitution itself." The fact pattern presented to the highest Court was simple, though dramatic, involving as it did a clash of conflicting sovereignties which, in most other systems, could be resolved only by force of arms. The Second Bank of the United States had been established by the Congress in 1816 to serve as a depository for federal funds and to print bank notes as a convenient medium of exchange. The state of Maryland had imposed a tax upon the Bank's Baltimore branch and the case arose out of an action against the cashier of this branch for the penalties prescribed for nonpayment of the tax.

The immediate issue before the Court was that of whether the Maryland law was constitutional. To decide it, the high bench had to probe into the very heart of national power under the Constitution and the relation between states and nation under the supremacy clause. As Marshall stated at the very outset of his opinion, "a sovereign state, denies the obligation of a law . . . of the Union. . . . The constitution of our country, in its most interesting and vital parts, is to be considered; the conflicting powers of the government of the Union and of its members . . . are to be discussed; and an opinion given, which may essentially influence the great operations of the government."

Marshall first took up the question of whether Congress had the power to charter a bank. The difficulty arose from the constitutional truism that the Federal Government is a government only of enumerated powers. "Among the enumerated powers," Marshall concedes, "we do not find that of establishing a bank or creating a corporation." But that did not, in his view, end the matter, for there is nothing in the Constitution which "excludes incidental or implied powers; and which requires that everything granted shall be expressly and minutely described." On the contrary, Article I, section 8, after enumerating the specific powers conferred on Congress, authorizes the national legislature "to make all laws which shall be necessary and proper for carrying into execution the foregoing powers, and all other powers vested by this Constitution in the government of the United States. . . ."

From the necessary-and-proper clause of Article I, section 8, Marshall (following Hamilton's celebrated bank message) derived the doctrine of implied powers, which has since become a basic part of our constitutional law. If the establishment of a national bank would aid the government in its exercise of its granted powers, the authority to set one up would be implied. "Let the end be legitimate," reads the key sentence of the Marshall opinion, "let it be within the scope of the constitution, and all means which are appropriate, which are plainly adapted to that end, which are not prohibited, but consist with the letter and spirit of the constitution, are constitutional."

Marshall's epochal opinion in *McCulloch v. Maryland* resolved the controversy that raged in the early days of the Republic between those who favored a strict construction and those who supported a broad construction of the necessary-and-proper clause. Conclusively put to rest was the view that the clause extended only to laws which were indispensably necessary. As construed by Marshall, the clause (aptly termed the "sweeping clause" at the time of the adoption of the Constitution) has been the fount and origin of vast federal authority. In truth, practically every power of the national government has been expanded in some degree by the clause.

Since the Bank of the United States was validly established by Congress, it followed logically that it could not be subjected to state taxation. The national government, declared Marshall, "is supreme within its sphere of action. This would seem to result necessarily from its nature." Such supremacy is utterly inconsistent with any state authority to tax a federal agency. "The question is, in truth, a question of supremacy; and if the right of the states to tax the means employed by the general government be conceded, the declaration that the constitution, and the laws made in pursuance thereof, shall be the supreme law of the land, is empty and unmeaning declamation."

In *McCulloch v. Maryland,* Marshall construed the basic document in the grand manner, in accordance with his own dictum there that we must never forget that "it is a *constitution* we are expounding"—a living instrument that must be interpreted so as to meet the practical needs of government. By refusing to bind the nation within the literal confines of its granted powers, he enabled it to grow and meet governmental problems which could not have been foreseen by the Framers.

The 1824 case of *Gibbons v. Ogden* gave Marshall the opportunity to deliver the classic opinion on the most important substantive power vested in the nation, at least in time of peace: the power "To regulate commerce with foreign nations, and among the several States. . . ." The need to federalize regulation of commerce, we saw in the last chapter, was one of the principal needs which motivated the men of 1787. Yet they were interested mainly in the negative aspects of such regulation, concerned as they were with curbing state restrictions which had oppressed and degraded the commerce of the nation. It was Marshall, in *Gibbons v. Ogden,* who first construed the commerce clause in a positive manner, enabling it to be fashioned into a formidable federal regulatory tool.

The case of *Gibbons v. Ogden* itself arose out of the invention of the steamboat by Robert Fulton. The New York legislature granted to the inventor and Robert Livingston the exclusive right to navigate the waters of that state by steam-propelled vessels. Aaron Ogden had secured a license from Fulton and Livingston to operate steamboats between New York and New Jersey. Thomas Gibbons started to operate his own steamboat line between the same two states in defiance of the New York-granted monopoly, though his boats were enrolled and licensed to engage in the coasting trade under an act of Congress. Ogden secured an injunction in a New York court to restrain Gibbons from operating within New York waters in violation of the state-granted monopoly.

By availing ourselves of the perspective of a century and a half of hindsight, we may assert today that the issue presented to Marshall and his colleagues in *Gibbons v. Ogden* was basically a simple one. Though Gibbons was operating his steamboats in violation of the New York monopoly, he was acting pursuant to a federal license permitting his vessels to engage in the coasting trade. Under these circumstances, the monopoly law of New

York came into collision with the federal licensing law and deprived Gibbons of the right to which the federal law entitled him.

If *Gibbons v. Ogden* stood only for the elementary proposition that a state law incompatible with an act of Congress must fall, the opinion there would hardly justify its characterization by Beveridge as "that opinion which has done more to knit the American people into an indivisible Nation than any other one force in our history, excepting only war." *Gibbons v. Ogden* stands as a constitutional landmark because both counsel and Court did not confine themselves to the narrow issue of conflict between state and federal law. Instead, the occasion was seized for a full-scale discussion of the scope of the commerce power.

The commerce clause vests in the Congress the power "to regulate commerce." The noun "commerce" determines the subjects to which congressional power extends. The verb "regulate" determines the type of authority that the Congress can exert. Both the noun and the verb were defined most broadly in Marshall's opinion.

"Commerce," in Marshall's view, covered all intercourse—a conception comprehensive enough to include within its scope all business dealings: "It describes the commercial intercourse between nations, and parts of nations, in all its branches."

Having given such a broad construction to the noun "commerce," Marshall proceeded to take an equally liberal view of the meaning of the verb "regulate." "What is this power?" he asked. "It is the power to regulate; that is, to prescribe the rule by which commerce is to be governed. This power, like all others vested in congress is complete in itself, may be exercised to its utmost extent. . . ."

As thus construed by Marshall, the commerce clause was to become the source of the most important powers which the Federal Government exercises in time of peace. If, in recent years, it has become almost trite to point out how regulation from Washington has come to guard and control us from the cradle to the grave, that is true only because of Marshall's emphasis at the outset upon what the Supreme Court, in our own day, has termed the embracing and penetrating nature of the commerce clause.

Marshall's principal opinions were summarized by his biographer as follows: In *Marbury v. Madison,* he established the fundamental principle of liberty, that a permanent, written Constitution controls a temporary Congress; in *McCulloch v. Maryland* and *Cohens v. Virginia,* he made the government of the American people a living thing; in *Gibbons v. Ogden,* he welded that people into a unit by the force of their commercial interests.

There are those, however, who deny that it really made a difference to the constitutional history of the nation that John Marshall, rather than some other man, held the highest judicial office when he did. When Justice Holmes observed that Marshall's "greatness consists in his *being* there," the implication was that any other judge, called upon to preside over the highest bench in the formative era of our constitutional law, would have filled the place as well.

We need not, in Justice Frankfurter's phrase, subscribe to the hero theory of history to recognize that great men do make a difference, even in the law. It was John Marshall who transformed the Supreme Court into the vital center of the constitutional system and laid down the legal foundation of an effective Union. It was his ability and personality that enabled him to accomplish these ends. Had he not sat when he did in the high bench's central chair, it is most unlikely that they would have been accomplished. Nor is such a statement mere conjecture. But for the circumstance that the responsibility of appointing the Chief Justice fell to John Adams, instead of to Jefferson a month later, the seminal expounder of the basic document would have been anyone but a man of Marshall's views.

The historian can state with confidence that the Marshall conception of the Constitution was a necessary prerequisite to the achievement of the nation's manifest destiny. Among Marshall's contemporaries, however, there was no such unanimous assurance. Marshall's views on the review power of the Supreme Court, as well as his basic nationalistic tenets, were bitterly opposed by most members of the dominant political party, including Spencer Roane, the Virginia judge whom, it is said, Jefferson would have appointed in Marshall's place.

To us, a century and a half later, the broad construction of the commerce power was plainly essential to the period of growth upon which the nation was entering. To the men of Marshall's day, the need was not nearly so obvious. To appreciate the very real contribution to national power made by *Gibbons v. Ogden,* we must contrast the opinion there with the restricted scope which President Monroe had just given to the commerce power in the 1822 veto of the Cumberland Road Act. According to Monroe, "A power . . . to impose . . . duties and imposts in regard to foreign nations and to prevent any on the trade between the States, was the only power granted." Marshall's sweeping opinion ruthlessly brushes aside this narrow theory. That Marshall was able to mold his intense convictions on effective national power into positive law at the outset surely made a difference to the ordered development of the nation.

More than that, Marshall's judicial genius enabled him to lay down the foundations of our constitutional law in terms that have endured. It is difficult to read one of Marshall's great opinions without being converted to its views. Listen to Benjamin N. Cardozo, himself no mean master of the judicial craft, speaking of Marshall's opinions:

> We hear the voice of the law speaking by its consecrated ministers with the calmness and assurance that are born of a sense of mastery and power. Thus Marshall seemed to judge, and a hush falls upon us even now as we listen to his words. Those organ tones of his were meant to fill cathedrals, or the most exalted of tribunals. . . . The thrill is irresistible. We feel the mystery and the awe of inspired revelation. His greatest judgments are framed upon this plane of exaltation and aloofness. The movement from premise to conclusion is put before the observer as something more impersonal than the working of the individual mind. It is the inevitable progress of an inexorable force.

Even Marshall's strongest critics were affected by the illusion. "All wrong, all wrong," we are told was the despairing comment of John Randolph of Roanoke, "but no man in the United States can tell why or wherein."

As we look at Marshall's work now, it is all too easy to say that it was only the product of the fortunate circumstance that it was done while the Constitution was still plastic and malleable. But the truth is that the cases decided by Marshall were great because of what he made of them. Any of them could have been decided in narrow, technical ways that would have left them all but unheard of outside the law courts. If today they are landmarks of the law, it is because they were raised to the elect plane by the great Chief Justice's transforming touch.

IV

STATES VERSUS NATION

ONE OF the most dramatic and interesting scenes in our history, Woodrow Wilson tells us, was that enacted on March 4, 1829, when Andrew Jackson was sworn into the Presidency by John Marshall, the aged Chief Justice at whose hands the law of the nation had received both its majesty and its spirit of ordered progress. "The two men," writes Wilson, "were at the antipodes from one another both in principle and in character; had no common insight into the institutions of the country which they served; represented one the statesmanship of will and the other the statesmanship of control."

To Marshall, Jackson's inauguration was a gloomy portent of the fate that awaited alike his constitutional labors and the effective national government which he sought to construct through them. "To men who think as you and I do," wrote Marshall to Joseph Story during the last year of his life, "the present is gloomy enough; and the future presents no cheering prospect." Toward the end of his career, the great Chief Justice saw the Supreme Court defied, both by the state of Georgia and the President. "John Marshall has made his decision," Jackson is reported to have said of the 1831 case of *Cherokee Nation v. Georgia,* "now let him enforce it!" The President, too, was the author of a vehement attack upon *McCulloch v. Maryland* and the very basis of the Supreme Court's review power in his message in 1832 vetoing a bill to extend the charter of the Bank of the United States. Well might Marshall feel that his long effort to construct judicial power as the cornerstone of an effective and enduring Union had been all but in vain.

Marshall's misgivings appeared justified when, after his death, Roger B. Taney was appointed to the high bench's central chair. Taney it was who had drafted the key portions of Jackson's veto message on the bill to renew the Bank of the United States and who had carried out the President's plan for the removal of government deposits from the Bank. When Marshall died, we are told by Robert G. McCloskey, the anguish of his admirers was compounded partly of grief for a beloved national figure and partly of apprehension that Jackson would select Taney to succeed him. Indeed, Daniel Webster wrote, after the appointment of Marshall's successor, "Judge Story . . . thinks the Supreme Court is *gone,* and I think so too."

To those who lived during Marshall's last days, the passing of the old order may have been something to be awaited with foreboding. The historian more than a century later can see that their fears were excessive. Even during Marshall's lifetime, despite the rebuffs of his later years, it should have been evident to the discerning observer that the doctrines of national power which the Chief Justice had espoused were bound to prevail in the era of expansion upon which the United States had entered.

That the need to mold constitutional principles to meet the demands of the westward movement would carry before it inconsistent constitutional doctrines had been demonstrated dramatically in the Louisiana Purchase of 1803. The extension of the American domain was brought about by Thomas Jefferson, despite the fact that, strict constructionist that he was, he had grave doubts that the Constitution vested in the nation any power to annex territory. The imperative needs of the nation forced Jefferson to lay his scruples aside. Thus he had to deal with the opportunity given by Napoleon's offer by methods as vigorous as any ever embraced by Hamilton. That the Supreme Court, through Marshall, was later to confirm in the law the inherent power of the nation to acquire property does not change the impact of Jefferson's act upon the doctrine of narrow construction, of which he had, from the beginning, been the principal exponent. When that doctrine stood in the way of the nation's destiny, it was silently discarded, even by its author, in favor of the theory of federal power espoused by Hamilton and Marshall.

The acquisition of Louisiana provided a tremendous impetus to the growth of nationalistic spirit in the United States. The nation itself was doubled in size and the treaty of cession expressly provided that the new territory should be admitted into the Union, "according to the principles of the Federal Constitution." This continuation of the enlightened policy of the Northwest Ordinance furnished powerful political inducement to would-be settlers, for it meant that they would be making new states, not merely populating colonies to be controlled by the "mother country" along the eastern seaboard. With the end of the War of 1812, people began to pour westward. Areas that had only a generation earlier been untracked wilderness were transformed into self-governing territories and then into full-fledged members of the Union. The American people had entered unreservedly into the historic task of occupying a continent.

All commentators agree that the Treaty of Ghent in 1814 coincided with a great upsurge in nationalism in most of the Union. The war frustrations had emphasized the dangers of weakening the Federal Government and Jackson's victory at New Orleans had graphically demonstrated what a strong nation might accomplish. The second war with Britain may have achieved none of the ostensible objects for which it was fought. Yet it did, as Albert Beveridge puts it, de-Europeanize America; it emancipated the nation from the intellectual and spiritual sovereignty of the Old World. In its place, a purely American spirit was developed, with an emphasis upon pride in nation that had not been seen or felt since the Revolution.

The new nationalism was particularly apparent in the developing West. The spirit and character of the frontiersman, in McLaughlin's characterization, made themselves felt even within the field of constitutional history. The West was naturally nationalistic, for expansion and nationalism are boon companions.

One can go further and state that the settlement of the new territories placed the imprimatur of history upon the constitutional theories of John Marshall. It was in the older states, with their histories and distinctive personalities antedating the Union by so many years, that it was possible to be an extreme exponent of states' rights. Parochialism is understandable in provinces which possess something of the magic of Athens and Rome and Florence. But it hardly made the same sense in regions which owed their very existence to the fostering guardianship of the Union. It was as wards of the nation that the new settlements grew into territories and finally into states. The westward shift of the national balance meant the inevitable end of the old provincialism.

The vast extent of the newly developed areas was a powerful stimulus to a nationalistic construction of the Constitution. "The valley of the Ohio," says Henry James, "had no more to do with that of the Hudson, the Susquehanna, the Potomac, the Roanoke, and the Santee, than the valley of the Danube with that of the Rhone, the Po, or the Elbe. Close communication by land could alone hold the great geographical divisions together." Such close communication could only be provided, as a practical matter, through internal improvements financed from Washington. Hence, the genesis of the so-called American System, which contemplated an extensive scheme of federal aid to achieve the execution of a comprehensive plan for roads and canals, designed to improve communications between the older and the newer areas of population. The Cumberland Road, begun before the War of 1812 to provide a great highway to the West, showed what could be done by a nation resolved to exercise its powers to minimize the physical distances between its parts.

The proposals to have the Federal Government participate directly in the building of internal improvements gave rise to serious constitutional controversy. The adherents of strict construction denied that the nation possessed such power in the absence of express provision therefor. But the imperative need to improve communications caused the advocates of national power ultimately to prevail. "Time and experience," declared Lincoln in the circular letter of 1832 which began his political career, "have verified to a demonstration the public utility of internal improvements." The sentiment thus expressed was that of the entire nation beyond the Alleghenies and was, in the long run, to prove irresistible. Veto messages by Madison and Monroe could do no more than delay the inevitable. And even Monroe came to admit the existence of federal power—at least for improvements which were general, rather than local, in character.

The change in Monroe's attitude opened the way to the federal financing of internal improvements. The constitutional justification was the Marshall doctrine of implied powers, which proved the legal key to the needs of an expanding Republic. The basic document, framed for thirteen seaboard states, was thus fitted to the requirements of a continent. As Henry Clay said, in a celebrated speech urging the liberal construction needed to justify federal road-building in the West, "We . . . are not legislating for this moment only, or for the present generation, or for the present populated limits of these States; but our acts must embrace a wider scope—reaching northwesterly to the Pacific."

It was hardly to be expected that all the older regions of the Union would watch with equanimity the westward march of the national center of gravity. On the contrary, many among those who remained along the Atlantic coast line observed the shift in power from the older to the newer regions of the Union with growing anxiety and dismay. To those who looked upon the expansion of the nation only as the cause of the diminution of their own influence, it was not unnatural to condemn the constitutional doctrines which furnished the legal basis for national growth. Such doctrines were challenged as heresy introduced into the fundamental law contrary to the intent of the Framers. In their place, reliance was placed upon a theory of the Constitution wholly opposed to the nationalistic conception espoused by Marshall. This theory emphasized, not national power, but the rights of the states, and was based upon the supposed sovereignty of the component parts of the Union.

The doctrine of state rights was one that was destined, from the beginning, to play a vital part in American constitutional history. Indeed, the dominant question from 1789 until the Civil War was whether such a doctrine would carry before it the concept of effective Union upon which the organic document was based.

The extreme exponents of state rights relied essentially on the claim that the states were separate sovereignties whose basic rights had not been impaired by adherence to the Union. From the claim of state sovereignty have flowed most attempts to frustrate the central governmental structure created by the Framers. Upon it have been based the doctrines of interposition, nullification, and secession, which at various times in American history have been urged against exercises of federal authority. The foundation of these doctrines was the assertion that the Constitution was a mere compact among the several states, which left them with sovereignty unimpaired, free to meet federal power with their own authority.

That the notion of the states as separate sovereignties contained the seeds of dissolution of the Union was seen as early as 1788 by Charles C. Pinckney, himself one of the Framers. "Let us then consider," he stated with profound insight, "all attempts to weaken this union by maintaining, that each state is separately and individually independent, as a species of political heresy, which can never benefit us, but may bring on us the most serious distresses."

Pinckney's foresight has been borne out throughout American history. Soon after the Constitution itself went into operation, the doctrine of state sovereignty was put forward as a means of frustrating federal power. The immediate cause was the enactment by the Congress in 1798 of the now notorious Alien and Sedition Acts. Feeling ran high against these laws in many states; they were considered an unwarranted invasion of constitutional rights, and their opponents determined to take a positive stand. The result was the Kentucky and Virginia Resolutions of 1798 and 1799, which were drafted by Jefferson and Madison, respectively.

The 1798 resolutions were based upon the concept of the Constitution as a compact between sovereign states: "That to this compact each State acceded as a State, and is an integral party." From this it followed that the states "are not united on the principle of unlimited submission to their General Government." On the contrary, "the Government created by this compact was not made the final judge of the extent of the powers delegated to itself." Instead, "as in all other cases of compact among parties having no common Judge, each party has an equal right to judge for itself, as well of infractions as of the mode and measure of redress."

A year later, provoked by reply resolutions from a number of Northern states rejecting their position, Jefferson and Madison drafted second resolutions which reiterated their position in even stronger form. The 1799 Virginia Resolution, after repeating the compact theory, went on to declare that, in case of deliberate, palpable, and dangerous exercise of other powers, not granted by the said compact, "the States who are parties thereto have the right, and are in duty bound, to interpose for arresting the progress of the evil, and for maintaining, within their respective limits, the authorities, rights, and liberties appertaining to them."

The second Kentucky Resolution went even further, proclaiming "that a Nullification, by those sovereignties, of all unauthorized acts done under color of that instrument, is the rightful remedy."

"Interposition," "nullification"—these were extreme doctrines which were utterly incompatible with the perpetual, more perfect Union envisaged by the Framers. Jefferson and Madison themselves, it is now recognized, did not really mean to go so far as some of their unguarded language appeared to indicate; indeed Madison, some thirty years later, expressly indicated that such was in fact the case. As Esmond Wright puts it, their purpose was as much propagandist as were the laws they were attacking themselves. At the same time, it can scarcely be gainsaid that the resolutions drafted by them planted the seeds of logic from which the later doctrines of Calhoun and Jefferson Davis grew. In the Kentucky and Virginia Resolutions, Edward S. Corwin informs us, the extreme state-rights outlook received a constitutional creed which in time was to become, at least in the South, a gloss upon the basic document regarded as authoritative as the original Constitution itself.

It is true that the first use in practice of the Kentucky-Virginia creed was in the New England states during the War of 1812. The Hartford Convention itself was based squarely upon the compact theory of the Constitution. Yet that was a mere temporary aberration, caused by the harsh impact upon the Northeast of the embargo and the war. The ending of the conflict with Britain made it readily apparent that the true interest of New England lay in an effective Union. It should not be forgotten that one of the principal planks in the American System urged by the proponents of nationalism amounted to a subsidy to Yankee manufacturers in the form of a protective tariff.

The tariff was a natural complement of the program for internal improvements. Provision of an improved system of transportation at government expense was intended to increase the self-sufficiency and strength of the nation. The same aim would also be served by nurture of the war-born industries of the Northeast. And a nation which possessed the constitutional power to carry out the plan to "bind the Republic together" would have like authority to enact tariff legislation.

But the tariff, originally intended only as a temporary measure to enable American industry to be placed on a competitive basis with that of Britain, proved increasingly obnoxious to the agricultural states of the South. When their hopes for tariff reform were defeated by enactment of the tariff of 1828—known to the South as the Tariff of Abominations—the Southerners had recourse to the creed enunciated in the Kentucky and Virginia Resolutions. The result was the first great constitutional conflict between states and nation—one which foreshadowed both the life-and-death struggle of a quarter century later and the ultimate victory of the nationalistic conception of the Union.

The tariff of 1828 led to the publication of the so-called *South*

Carolina Exposition by the legislature of that state. Drafted by John C. Calhoun, it affirmed and justified the right of the states to interpose their own authority and nullify acts of the Federal Government. Although the legislature ordered the *Exposition* printed, it did not formally adopt it. Instead, in resolutions, it protested against the constitutionality of the tariff system and expressed "the hope that the magnanimity and justice of the good people of the Union will affect the abandonment of a system, partial in its nature, unjust in its operation, and not within the powers delegated to Congress."

The nation was, however, unwilling in this respect to make concessions to the South. The Tariff Act of 1832 indicated to Calhoun and the other leaders of the nullifying party that the only way out was through practical implementation of the theory advanced in the *Exposition.* In the words of the South Carolina delegation to Congress, after passage of the 1832 act, the situation left "the question of remedy to the sovereign power of the state."

In the meantime, the basic issue involved had been dramatically crystallized for the people by the celebrated senatorial debate between Daniel Webster and Robert Hayne in 1830. Hayne had articulated what were fundamentally the Calhoun theories of state sovereignty and nullification. Webster replied in classic terms, which were essentially a restatement of the Marshall doctrine of the nature of the Union. It may, indeed, be said that it was Webster's florid oratory that gave popular currency to the theory of national power expounded in Marshall's opinions.

Webster, like the great Chief Justice had done before him, effectively repudiated the notion of the states as separate sovereignties which had established the Union as their agent. The Federal Government, he emphatically demonstrated, "is not the creature of the State Governments." But the time had passed for mere argument, however sound in logic, to play the decisive role. The nullification party in South Carolina had won the state election of 1832 and prepared to prevent the execution of the new tariff law.

The South Carolina government proceeded to give effect to the Calhoun theory by organizing a convention, which promptly convened and passed the so-called Nullification Ordinance. In the name of "We . . . the People of South Carolina," it declared the tariff acts of 1828 and 1832 "unauthorized by the Constitution of the United States . . . and null, void and no law, nor binding upon this State, its officers, or citizens." It further declared it unlawful for federal or state officials to attempt to enforce the acts; prohibited appeals to the United States Supreme Court in cases arising under the ordinance; and required all state officials to take an oath to obey and enforce the ordinance. In addition, it was proclaimed that efforts on the part of the nation to enforce the nullified laws by force would be "inconsistent with the longer continuance of South Carolina in the Union," and would absolve that state from "their political connection with the people of the other States."

Calhoun and his followers may well have believed that implementation of the nullification doctrine did not necessarily involve the use of force on either side. Such a belief (if it existed) was nevertheless contrary to the effective realities of the situation. Nullification was utterly inconsistent with continued preservation of the nation. Its establishment as an accepted doctrine would have meant the end of the Union ordained by the Framers almost as much as the secessions that took place in 1861. The Federal Government, so long as it was to remain a true government, was bound to meet the South Carolina ordinance with the threat of forceful action. Then—unless either or both sides gave way—the ultimate decision, as the events of a quarter century later were to show, could only be left to the arbitrament of arms.

Contemporary admirers of the constitutional edifice erected by Marshall might look upon Andrew Jackson as the instrument chosen for its destruction. But Jackson as President was, paradoxical though it may sound, far from an unswerving adherent to all the theoretical principles of Jacksonian democracy. Product of the West that he was, he owed his primary allegiance to the United States. More than that, elected as a popular leader, he resolved to use the executive power to carry out the program of his party. He saw clearly, as Amaury de Riencourt states it, that the President's stature rose with that of the nation. When confronted with the South Carolina ordinance, which threatened to result in the very dissolution of the nation, Jackson replied in emphatic terms in a proclamation affirming his adherence to a strong union.

The Jackson proclamation did not mince words in taking up the challenge thrown down by the nullifiers. The power asserted by South Carolina, it unequivocally declared, "is incompatible with the existence of the Union, contradicted expressly by the letter of the Constitution, unauthorized by its spirit, inconsistent with every principle on which it was founded, and destructive of the great object for which it was formed."

Nor did Jackson restrict himself to restatement of the nationalistic view of the Union. In addition, he emphasized that the President had no discretion with regard to execution of the nation's laws: "my duty is emphatically pronounced in the Constitution. Those who told you that you might peaceably prevent their execution deceived you."

The President's strong feelings on the matter were not limited to words. He sent a warship and seven revenue cutters to Charleston Harbor. In addition, we are told in Van Buren's *Autobiography* that Jackson was actually inclined to go to South Carolina at the head of a *posse comitatus* to arrest the nullification leaders, "and deliver them to the Judicial power of the United States to be dealt with according to law."

The President then reported the situation to Congress and requested additional powers to enforce federal law. Congress responded with the Force Act of 1833. It empowered the Chief Executive to employ force, where necessary, to secure the execution within a state of federal statutes. At the same time, however, the advocates of compromise on Capitol Hill were able to secure enactment of a new tariff act, which provided for a gradual reduction in duties. The compromise tariff avoided the need for national power to be put to the test of arms. South Carolina repealed the Nullification Ordinance; though, to even the balance, it also went through the formal procedure of "nullifying" the Force Act itself.

The ultimate conflict between state and national power was thus postponed for three decades. Yet, if to many South Carolinians, the outcome of the nullification controversy was a victory for their state, their view lost sight of the realities of the situation. If South Carolina had championed the extreme Calhoun theories, she had stood alone in doing so. Even the Southern states which were also hostile to the tariff had not significantly supported the South Carolina stand.

Arrayed on the other side, at the same time, had been the combined power of all three branches of the national government. The Force Act had passed the Congress with overwhelming majorities. And it placed the national legislature on record with the executive and judicial branches in favor of the nationalistic view of the Union. "All this," concludes Andrew McLaughlin in his constitutional history, "furnishes a pretty strong support of the prevalent belief that the government was a real government and could enforce its laws even though a state *in convention* attempted to nullify them."

Of especial significance in this respect was the strong position taken by President Jackson. "The Proclamation, but more especially the Message, adopt all your principles," affirmed a letter written to Daniel Webster early in 1833. Jackson may have been elected with Southern votes, but he knew that the destiny of the American people could be fulfilled only under a strong union. Disunion, he asserted in his proclamation, is treason. Two years before his death, John Marshall was thus to see the vindication of his nationalistic doctrines in the words of the President whom he had considered their greatest adversary.

Jackson, at the same time, did more than lend verbal support to the great Chief Justice's conception of national supremacy. Jacksonian democracy meant a revitalization of the highest office, which transformed the President into both the tribune of the people and the effective head of the national administration. This was to lay the foundation for the powerful Executive without which a strong nation could scarcely exist.

From a constitutional point of view, the Jackson contribution to the development of the Presidency arose out of his actions with regard to two essential presidential powers: the veto power and the removal power.

Before Jackson, there had been no effective use of the authority to negative laws. That was true because the early Presidents, following the view expressed by Jefferson in 1791, had acted on the assumption that the veto power was to be used only as a defense against unconstitutional legislation. Jackson brushed aside this restrictive theory, and acted instead on the belief that the President might interpose his negative on any grounds deemed by him desirable. His opponents complained that Jackson's vetoes, particularly that of the bill for rechartering the Second United States Bank, were unconstitutional. Yet Jackson's vetoes clearly put to rest the legal issue and settled the power of the President to veto bills which he deemed objectionable on their merits or for any other reasons which might commend themselves to him.

Even more important in its practical impact upon the development of the Presidency was Jackson's establishment in practice of his removal power. The main functions of a Chief Executive fall into two principal categories: political and administrative. In different countries the emphasis laid upon each of these functions varies. In some, the powers and influence of the head of the executive are almost entirely political. In others, such as Switzerland, the chief function is administrative.

In the United States today, we see a striking concentration in the President of all the executive power vested in the Federal Government. It is, however, arguable that this concentration is one that was not contemplated by the Framers. In their conception, the President was intended to be essentially a political and military chief. The officers in charge of administrative affairs were intended to be, not under his direction, but under the direction of, and accountable to, the Congress.

The very first Congress, in organizing the federal administration, acted upon the conception just stated. In setting up the Departments of Foreign Affairs and War, having to do with political and military matters, the Congress placed them under the control of the President. When it came to the formation of the Treasury Department, on the other hand, Congress showed a clear purpose to keep the department's administration under Congress's own direction. The same intent may be seen in the

1794 law organizing the Post Office, the second great administrative department.

Yet, if the first Congress intended to vest the administrative primacy in itself, it in large part nullified that objective by a crucial vote on the removal power. In establishing the Department of Foreign Affairs, Congress, after lengthy debate on the matter, provided for removal from office of the head of the new department by the President.

According to the Supreme Court in a leading 1926 case, the "decision of 1789" (as the vote in the first Congress on the removal power has been termed) was, and was intended to be, a legislative declaration that the power to remove all department heads was vested in the President alone. The use of such power in practice was strikingly demonstrated in 1833 by President Jackson. Jackson had ordered Secretary of the Treasury Duane to transfer federal funds from the Bank of the United States. Duane refused to comply. He was forthwith removed from office by the President. His successor, Roger B. Taney, then immediately effected the fund transfer which Jackson had directed.

It has been said that Jackson's removal of Duane has had more value as a precedent than even a score of judicial decisions. It all but conclusively settled the position of the President as the administrative chief of the government. The President, as a practical matter, has the power to force any department head to do any act which that official has authority to do. He can dictate in all matters because of his power of instant dismissal. In this respect, might makes right within the executive branch. What the President commands will be done by executive officials—at least if they wish to retain their appointments.

From Jackson's day (with the exception of the experience under Andrew Johnson), the removal power has been the sanction that has enabled the President to secure his position as effective head of the national administration. Nor can it be denied that the actual development in this respect has been a most salutary one. The experience under the Articles of Confederation demonstrates the utter impracticability of administration subject to the sole direction of the legislature. Such administration is bound to result in feeble execution of the laws. With the concentration in the President of the powers of chief administrator, the debility inherent in headless administration can be avoided.

The judicial branch, too, under Jackson and his successors, continued the constitutional work begun by Marshall and his colleagues. If we look at the constitutional work of Roger B. Taney, avoiding a tendency to compare his accomplishments with the colossal structure erected by his predecessor, we find it far from a mean contribution to the organic development of the nation. The shadow of the *Dred Scott* decision, it is now generally recognized, for too long cast an unfair shadow over Taney's judicial stature.

To be sure, there was an inevitable reaction after Marshall's death; but it was not nearly as great as has often been supposed. Chief Justice Taney may not have been as nationalistic in his beliefs as his predecessor. Yet, under him also, the basic theme of constitutional development was that of formulation of the principles needed to insure the expansion and survival of the Union.

Of particular interest to one concerned with the work of the Taney Court is its contribution toward the commercial expansion of the nation. The industrial growth which has so strikingly altered the nature of American society during the past century would scarcely have been possible had it depended solely upon the initiative and resources of the individual entrepreneur. It has been the corporate device that has enabled men to establish the pools of wealth and the talent needed for the economic conquest of a continent.

It should, however, be borne in mind that the corporation is entirely a creation of the law, whose very existence and legal personality must needs have its origin in some act of the law. The corporation as a legal person was developed under the precolonial English law. As such, it was recognized from the beginning in American law—especially in the classic 1819 *Dartmouth College v. Woodward* decision. But it was not until Taney's opinion in the leading case of *Bank of Augusta v. Earle* (1839) that the corporate device could be made to serve the needs of the burgeoning American economy. The decision of the lower federal court there had held that a corporation created in one state had no power to make a contract or to act in any other matter in another state. Such a ruling, which, in effect, limited corporations to the doing of business only in the states in which they were chartered, would have rendered all but impossible the growth of interstate business enterprises of any consequence. Well might Daniel Webster, in his argument, characterize it as "anti-commercial and anti-social . . . and calculated to break up the harmony which has so long prevailed among the States and People of this Union."

The Taney opinion rejected the notion that a corporation could have no existence beyond the limits of the state in which it was chartered. On the contrary, it held that a corporation, like a natural person, might act in states where it did not reside. Comity among the states provides a warrant for the operation throughout the Union of corporations chartered in any of the states.

Bank of Augusta v. Earle was the first step in what the Supreme Court in 1894 was to cite as "the constant tendency of judicial decisions in modern times . . . in the direction of putting corporations upon the same footing as natural persons." This tendency has been the essential jurisprudential counterpart of the economic unfolding of the nation.

The effect of the *Bank of Augusta* decision was as nationalistic as any of those rendered by Marshall himself. Webster could declare, after it was rendered, that "the Supreme Court is yet sound; and much as we cherish Whig victories, yet we cherish this conservative victory more; it is a triumph of the Constitution and Union again." The fear that the constitutional edifice constructed by Marshall was to be destroyed was, in large part, dispelled.

It is, nevertheless, erroneous to assume that the Taney Court was engaged merely in refurbishing the Marshall constitutional temple. Marshall had been concerned only with strengthening the powers of the fledgling nation so that it might realize its political and economic destiny throughout what he once termed "the American empire." Like the Framers themselves, he stressed the need to protect property rights as the essential prerequisite to such realization. By Taney's day, it came to be seen that private property, however important, was not the be-all and end-all of social existence. "While the rights of property are sacredly guarded," declared Taney in his very first important opinion for the high bench, "we must not forget that the community also have rights, and that the happiness and well being of every citizen depends on their faithful preservation."

Concern for the rights of the community, as well as those of the individual property owner, led to articulation by the Taney Court of the *police power*—one of the truly seminal concepts in our constitutional law. In the 1847 *License Cases,* the term "police powers" was used expressly to designate "nothing more or less than the powers of government inherent in every sovereignty to the extent of its dominions." It is by virtue of such power that a state may, "for the safety or convenience of trade, or for the protection of the health of its citizens," regulate the rights of property and person. Thenceforth, a principal task of the Supreme Court was to be the determination of the proper balance between the rights of the individual and the police power.

In a federal system, at the same time, it is equally important that a just balance be maintained between nation and states. In the field of constitutional law, this has been particularly true with regard to economic regulation. Marshall, with his expansive view of the commerce clause, had perhaps tilted the scale unduly in favor of national power—though even he, in a provocative opinion delivered near the end of his career, had implied that there was a range of permissible state authority over commerce. It was left to the Taney Court to raise the notion of concurrent state power over commerce to the level of accepted constitutional doctrine. More than that, such Court laid down a doctrinal line to determine when such state power might legitimately be exercised.

It did so in the 1851 case of *Cooley v. Board of Port Wardens*—a decision that bears the same relation to the subject of state power over commerce that *Gibbons v. Ogden* does to that of the federal commerce power. Before *Cooley,* the cases on the subject assumed a complete dichotomy between national and state authority over commerce: in all cases, either Congress must possess exclusive power or the states must be vested with coextensive, concurrent power. The *Cooley* decision, for the first time, expressly recognized that an either/or approach was not the only possible solution. Instead, said the Court, the question of whether there is exclusive federal power or concurrent state power as well depends upon the subjects of the power—and, in particular, upon whether they are of such a nature as to require exclusive legislation by Congress. Whether the states may regulate in such a case depends upon whether it is imperative that the subjects of the regulation be regulated by a uniform national system or whether, on the contrary, "it is likely to be the best provided for, not by one system, or plan of regulations, but by as many as the legislative discretion of the several States should deem applicable to the local peculiarities . . . within their limits."

The *Cooley* case has insured that, in drawing the judicial line between national and state power in the commerce field, due regard will be maintained for the values inherent in our federalism. Unless the subject of the power is such that it must be regulated uniformly throughout the nation from Washington alone, it may be regulated by each of the states to meet the differing needs posed by their local conditions and problems—at least, unless and until the Congress provides otherwise.

But, if the Taney Court was thus able to fix a balance between states and nation in the field of commercial regulation, the same was not true insofar as the basic question of sovereignty as between the states and the Federal Government was concerned. For, with regard to this question, the Constitution itself makes no provision for a balance between the two centers of government—but only for a preponderance of federal power within the expansive area assigned to the nation in Article I, section 8. When the Taney Court sought to do more than maintain the federal supremacy provided for by the Framers, its effort was foredoomed to failure.

This was particularly true of the attempt in the 1857 *Dred Scott* case to resolve in the judicial forum the basic controversy over slavery which had come to rend the nation asunder. The slavery question, said James Buchanan in his inaugural address a few days before the Supreme Court decision, "is a judicial question, which legitimately belongs to the Supreme Court of the United States, before whom it is now pending, and will, it is understood, be speedily and finally settled."

Armed with the perspective of a century of hindsight, we can see that in the *Dred Scott* case the Supreme Court fell a victim to its own success as a governmental institution. The power and prestige which had been built up under Marshall, and continued under Taney, had led men to expect too much of judicial power. The other branches had failed signally in resolving the issue which threatened to destroy the Union. What was more natural than to entrust the controversy to that august tribunal which had come to be looked upon as the vital fulcrum of the American system?

The Justices themselves, after much hesitation, too blithely accepted the notion that judicial power could succeed where political power had so manifestly failed. The *Dred Scott* decision seized the constitutional issue by ruling squarely on the thorniest aspect of the slavery controversy—the question of slavery in the territories. And it did so by holding that such a question was one that was beyond the power of the nation itself.

Taney's opinion for the Court in *Dred Scott* contained two main points. First of all, he ruled that Negroes were not and could not become citizens within the meaning of the Constitution. In addition, he rejected the claim that Scott had become a free man (and hence eligible for citizenship) by virtue of residence in a territory from which slavery had been excluded by the Missouri Compromise of 1820. This was true because "the act of Congress which prohibited a citizen from holding and owning property of this kind in the territory of the United States north of the line therein mentioned, is not warranted by the Constitution, and is therefore void."

There was more, of course, in the turgid opinion of the Chief Justice, as well as the seven other opinions rendered in the case. But what burst with such dramatic impact upon the nation was the fact that the highest Court in the land had denied both the right of Negroes to be citizens and the power of Congress to interfere with slaveholding in the territories. Acquiescence in such rulings was fatal alike to the Republicans and the advocates of popular sovereignty. It frustrated the hopes of those who sought to confine slavery to a section that would become an ever-smaller minority in an expanding nation. It meant instead that slavery itself was a national institution and that Congress could not abolish it in the territories. There was, in Bruce Catton's characterization, now no legal way in which slavery could be excluded from any territory.

Buchanan might declare, while *Dred Scott* was pending, "To their decision, in common with all good citizens, I shall cheerfully submit, whatever this may be." To the rest of the country, it was not that simple. A century later, we can see that they, rather than the President, were right. We now know that the charge of conspiracy and collusion between Buchanan, the Southerners in Congress, and the Justices, which many believed at the time, has no real basis. Yet we also realize that a question which resulted in a civil war was hardly a proper one for judicial resolution. It was, as Robert G. McCloskey points out, an essential mistake to imagine that a flaming political issue could be quenched by calling it a "legal" issue and deciding it judicially.

The *Dred Scott* decision itself had two direct results—though they were exactly the contrary of those which had been intended. In the first place, the storm of abuse which burst over the majority decision cast a dark shadow over the highest bench itself. No decision in our history, we are told, has done more to injure the reputation of the Supreme Court. For the better part of a generation thereafter, that tribunal was to remain in the shade, playing a diminished role in the governmental structure.

Yet the self-inflicted wound—grievous though it doubtless was—was not to prove fatal to the judicial institution. The need for an impartial umpire in a working constitutional federation was to prove too great. For the balance properly to be kept, judicial power could not for long remain in repose. The organic edifice erected by Marshall and Taney was too sound to be undermined by any one decision—however "reckless and disastrous" (Justice Robert H. Jackson's characterization) it might have been.

From an immediate point of view, even more important was

the effect of *Dred Scott* upon the political polarization of the nation. If anything, the decision had the opposite effect from that intended by those who had hoped by means of a Supreme Court pronouncement to quell the sectional strife that threatened to destroy the Union. Far from accomplishing this goal, *Dred Scott* actually proved a catalyst which helped precipitate the civil conflict that soon followed.

With the *Dred Scott* decision, graphically states the *American Heritage History of the Civil War,* "collapsed the whole elaborate house of cards which was sectional compromise." And with it collapsed the practical possibility of resolving by political and legal means the issues which divided the nation. Thenceforth the extremists on both sides were to dominate the scene. Bloodshed alone, as it turned out, could settle the slavery isue and the very nature of the Union which the issue had placed in the balance.

V

CONSTITUTIONAL CRUCIBLE

"DETERMINING the proper role to be assigned to the military in a democratic society," declared Chief Justice Earl Warren in his 1962 James Madison Lecture, "has been a troublesome problem for every nation that has aspired to a free political life." The claims of military power were first presented in extreme form in the American constitutional system during the Civil War. Nor can it be said that a proper balance between military power and law was achieved during that conflict. On the contrary, in the midst of civil strife most of all, as Edmund Burke pointed out in *Reflections on the French Revolution,* "Laws are commanded to hold their tongues amongst arms; and tribunals fall to the ground with the peace they are no longer able to uphold."

It was at the very outset of the Civil War that there were presented the extreme claims of both war and law in our system. The former was personified by President Lincoln, the latter by Chief Justice Taney. To deal with the life-and-death crisis which faced the government after the fall of Fort Sumter, Lincoln assumed powers no other President had exercised up to that time. On his own authority, he suspended the writ of *habeas corpus* and ordered wholesale arrests without warrants, detentions without trials, and imprisonments without judicial convictions. Private mail was opened and persons ordered arrested and held incommunicado by military officers acting under presidential authority. As Taney put it, the military had "thrust aside the judicial authorities and officers to whom the constitution has confided the power and duty of interpreting and administering the laws, and substituted a military government in its place, to be administered and executed by military officers."

The passage just quoted was part of an opinion delivered in May, 1861, by Taney, in the celebrated case of *Ex parte Merryman.* On April 27, 1861, President Lincoln authorized the Commanding General of the Army to suspend the right of *habeas corpus* along any military line between Philadelphia and Washington. A month later, Chief Justice Taney, sitting on circuit in Baltimore, was petitioned for *habeas corpus* by John Merryman, who had been arrested and confined in Fort McHenry by the Army for his secessionist activities, particularly his participation in the attack upon the Sixth Massachusetts Militia, while it was en route to Washington, and the destruction of railroad bridges to prevent the passage of troops. Sitting in chambers, Taney granted a writ of *habeas corpus* directed to the post commander. On the return date, an aide-de-camp, in full military uniform and appropriately wearing a sword and bright red sash, appeared in the courtroom and declined obedience to the writ, on the ground that it had been suspended by the Commanding General, pursuant to the April 27 order of the President.

Taney then delivered his *Merryman* opinion, in which he sharply condemned as illegal the suspension of *habeas corpus* by the President and the arrest, without warrant and hearing, of a civilian by military order. But Taney's vindication of the letter of the law against military claims of emergency was drowned out by cannon and marching feet. Taney's denial of presidential power to suspend *habeas corpus* had no practical consequence, since, as already noted, the military authorities concerned declined obedience to the court's writ. As the aged Chief Justice himself plaintively put it: "I have exercised all the power which the constitution and laws confer upon me, but that power has been resisted by a force too strong for me to overcome."

A century later, looking back at the conflict presented in *Merryman,* we can see that neither the Lincoln approach nor the Taney philosophy alone is adequate for the requirements of a war period. What is needed is some reconciliation of the extreme demands of war and law, not the complete exclusion of the one or the other. It was with keen perception that Justice Robert H. Jackson wrote, shortly before his death in 1954: "Had Mr. Lincoln scrupulously observed the Taney policy, I do not know whether we would have had any liberty, and had the Chief Justice adopted Mr. Lincoln's philosophy as the philosophy of the law, I again do not know whether we would have had any liberty."

It can hardly be denied that some of the measures taken by Lincoln during the Civil War, especially at the very outset of the conflict, went beyond constitutional legality. At the same time, it must be conceded that the situation which confronted the nation after Lincoln took office was one which the Framers could scarcely foresee. As William Dunning aptly characterized it half a century ago, "The circumstances in which the government found itself after the fall of Sumter were entirely unprecedented." Congress was not then in session, and immediate executive action to preserve the Union was called for.

In a series of proclamations, Lincoln asserted unparalleled authority—in effect amounting to presidential control over the war effort—until legislative approval could be obtained. He called out 75,000 of the militia under a statute which his predecessor had held did not give the President such power. Upon his own authority, "with a view . . . to the protection of public peace, and the lives and property of quiet and orderly citizens pursuing their lawful occupations," he proclaimed a blockade of the Southern ports. In other proclamations, he called for volunteers and enlarged the regular Army and Navy. In addition, as already seen, he ordered arrests by the military and suspension of the writ of *habeas corpus.* "In the interval between April 12 and July 4, 1861," says Dunning, "a new principle thus appeared in the constitutional system of the United States, namely, that of a temporary dictatorship. All the powers of government were virtually concentrated in a single department, and that the department whose energies were directed by the will of a single man."

It is true that the authority exercised by Lincoln was so sweeping that he has been characterized by a British observer as exercising "more arbitrary power than any Englishman since Oliver Cromwell." More than that, the power so exerted was, in the main, assumed by the President on his own authority, without express constitutional or statutory basis. In calling out the militia, to be sure, Lincoln was (despite the contrary opinion which Buchanan had expressed) acting within the powers given to him expressly by a 1795 act of Congress. Of more doubtful legality was much of his other action—particularly his measures to increase the personnel of the armed forces without congressional authorization. Lincoln himself recognized this. In reporting to Congress on his actions, on July 4, 1861, he stated, "These measures, whether strictly legal or not, were ventured upon under what appeared to be a popular demand and a public necessity; trusting then, as now, that Congress would readily ratify them."

Yet, if it may be doubted whether the Constitution confers upon the President, as well as the Congress, the power to raise armed forces, it should be borne in mind that Congress did enact a law in August, 1861, which expressly ratified Lincoln's actions. It provided that all of the President's acts respecting the Army and Navy and the calling out of the militia or volunteers "are hereby approved and in all respects legalized and made valid . . . as if they had been issued and done under the previous express authority and direction of the Congress."

Such ratification, the Supreme Court has ruled, gave to Lincoln's action full legal effect, just as though it had been authorized in advance by statute. Since, as Lincoln himself put it in his July 4 message, "nothing has been done beyond the constitutional competency of Congress," the congressional ratification made it possible to avoid the direct constitutional issue of the power of the President to act as he did, solely on his own authority.

In addition, even if we consider Lincoln's acts on his own authority alone, we must bear in mind the reality of the situation facing the nation after Sumter. The armed forces in the spring of 1861 numbered only some 13,000 men—a pitifully inadequate number to deal with the emergency. Unless the President himself took speedy and effective action, the Union might be ruptured beyond repair before the Congress could authorize the necessary measures. "The President," the highest Court itself affirmed in 1863, "was bound to meet it [i.e., the outset of the Civil War] in the shape it presented itself, without waiting for Congress to baptize it with a name; and no name given to it by him or them could change the fact."

To Lincoln, without a doubt, the idea of imposing legal shackles on the power to which the very existence of the nation was confided was one of those refinements which owed their origin to a zeal for liberty more ardent than enlightened. Even constitutional doctrine, he felt, might have to give way, if it conflicted with the national necessity. "By general law," he asserted at the height of what must still be considered our greatest national emergency, "life and limb must be protected, yet often a limb must be amputated to save a life; but a life is never wisely given to save a limb."

As already intimated, we need not today wholly accept the Lincoln philosophy with its practical subordination of the Constitution to the law of war. The proper approach, indeed, may be said to be somewhere between the extremes personified in 1861 by the great President and Chief Justice Taney. Under it, the basic document is treated as a plastic instrument, designed to meet all the possible circumstances with which the government set up under it may be confronted—including those which endanger its very being. As such, the Constitution itself is not suspended during any of the great exigencies of government—not even during a struggle for the very existence of the nation. But its provisions must be construed so as to give the nation the powers needed to preserve itself. This means that the Constitution in time of war is not to be regarded in exactly the same manner as that document in time of peace. The validity of action under the war power is to be judged wholly in the context of war. That action is not to be stigmatized as lawless because like action in time of peace would be lawless.

The Constitution, in this approach, depends for its application upon the factual circumstances which call its provisions into play.

It will thus be different in its application in time of war than in less pressing times. "Certain proceedings," as Lincoln himself stated in a noted 1863 letter, "are constitutional when in case of rebellion or invasion the public safety requires them, which would not be constitutional when, in the absence of rebellion or invasion, the public safety does not require them; in other words . . . the Constitution is not, in its application, in all respects the same in cases of rebellion or invasion involving the public safety, as it is in times of profound peace and public security."

Such an approach does not mean that the Constitution and the guaranteed rights of individuals contained therein may be overridden in wartime at the mere pleasure of the Executive. Yet it does justify the taking of action required by the exigencies of war which could not be permitted in more normal times. From this point of view, many of the measures taken by Lincoln to meet the emergency posed by the Civil War can be reconciled with the proper working of our constitutional law.

If there is difficulty in justifying any of Lincoln's actions from a constitutional point of view, it exists primarily with regard to his infringements upon civil liberties. One may, as already indicated, sustain the measures taken which relate to the affirmative waging of war, such as the raising of armed forces and the blockade of the South, on the ground that, without them, the military effort to preserve the Union would have perished stillborn. But must we necessarily say the same thing about patent violations of civil liberties which contravene clear organic provisions? Must transgressions upon personal liberty be condoned merely because of executive *ipse dixit?*

The issue of the legality of such executive transgressions was presented in dramatic form at the very outset of the Civil War in the *Merryman* case. At issue there was the question of whether the President could, on his own authority, direct the suspension of *habeas corpus* and hence effectively immunize military arrests and detentions from any judicial scrutiny. Chief Justice Taney's *Merryman* opinion represents an unqualified negative answer to this question. The claim that the President had the power to suspend the writ, said Taney, was one that he had listened to "with some surprise, for I had supposed it to be one of those points of constitutional law upon which there was no difference of opinion, and that it was admitted on all hands, that the privilege of the writ could not be suspended, except by act of congress."

Taney's conclusion with regard to the exclusive power of the Congress to suspend the writ was based in large part upon the fact that the constitutional clause relating to *habeas corpus* is located in Article I: "This article is devoted to the legislative department of the United States, and has not the slightest reference to the executive department." On the other hand, Article II, from which presidential power is derived, contains nothing on *habeas corpus* or its suspension. "And," according to Taney, "if the high power over the liberty of the citizen now claimed, was intended to be conferred on the president, it would undoubtedly be found in plain words in this article; but there is not a word in it that can furnish the slightest ground to justify the exercise of the power."

We have already seen that Taney's denial of presidential power had no practical consequence, since the military authorities concerned declined obedience to the court's writ. At the end of his opinion, Taney directed the clerk to send a copy of his opinion to the President. What Lincoln did with the copy sent to him remains undisclosed. But we do know that the *Merryman* opinion had little effect on the President's actions; Lincoln went right on exercising the power that the Chief Justice had branded as unconstitutional. In addition to other limited suspensions of the writ, such as that involved in *Merryman,* Lincoln issued an order on September 24, 1862, suspending *habeas corpus* throughout the country for all persons confined by military authority.

Some five months after the general suspension order just referred to, the Congress enacted an 1863 statute which expressly authorized the President to suspend the privilege of the writ of *habeas corpus,* in any part of the United States, "during the present rebellion . . . whenever, in his judgment, the public safety may require it." The Supreme Court itself has assumed the validity of the 1863 Act, both as a ratification of prior executive suspensions and as a delegation to the President of prospective power to suspend the writ.

The Habeas Corpus Act of 1863, viewed both as ratification and delegation, settled the immediate legal question of Lincoln's power to suspend the writ. Still the broader issue raised in the *Merryman* case—that of the President's power to suspend it in the absence of congressional authorization—remains. Until the Civil War, it was generally assumed that only the Congress could authorize suspension of *habeas corpus.* Chief Justice Taney confirmed this assumption in his *Merryman* opinion. Other federal and state cases decided during the Civil War take a similar view. The same has been true of most commentators upon the matter. From the Civil War down to our own day, the consensus of learned opinion has been that, on the legal issue involved in *Merryman,* Taney was right and Lincoln was wrong.

The same may be said about other comparable infringements upon personal liberty during the Civil War period, as well as violations of other civil liberties, such as the freedom of the press. The "suppression" of obnoxious newspapers, for example, finds no justification whatever in our law and can scarcely be excused by military necessity.

Yet, even with regard to what we should now regard as clear violations of the Constitution, certain things should be said, if not in justification, at least in explanation. It should, in the first place, be borne in mind that the line of demarcation between military and civil authority was much more blurred a century ago than it has since become. When Lincoln declared, in an 1863 letter, that "the Constitution invests its Commander-in-Chief with the law of war in time of war," he was stating what today would be considered constitutional heresy. But to the jurist of Lincoln's time, the constitutional wall of separation between military and civil power was by no means so settled. It should not be forgotten that all of the leading cases on the matter (starting with the 1866 *Milligan* case) were decided after Lincoln's actions had themselves become a matter of history.

With the law thus unsettled, it is perhaps not surprising that the Constitution was at times "stretched" at the expense of individual rights. Yet it should be borne in mind that most of the arbitrary measures in individual cases were acts of subordinates, not those of the President himself. In one of the extreme cases, for example, the arrest and detention of the outspoken Clement Vallandigham, the military commander concerned, General Burnside, acted in a manner which would, at the least, today be deemed questionable. In justifying his action to a federal judge, Burnside went so far as to ask, "Why should such speeches from our own public men be allowed? . . . They create dissensions and discord which, just now, amounts to treason" and indicated further that the distributors of demoralizing speeches should be "hung if found guilty."

But such was not Lincoln's view. As Gideon Welles's diary notes, "Good men . . . find it difficult to defend these acts. They are Burnside's, unprompted . . . by any member of the administration." He went on to observe, "The President . . . regrets what has been done." Over and over, J. G. Randall informs us, Lincoln had to intervene to caution and rebuke military commanders who went to extremes in overriding basic rights. Lincoln himself, we are told, was both surprised and distressed when he first learned of the facts in *causes célèbres* like the *Vallandigham* case.

In assessing the constitutional crisis presented during the Civil War, the important thing to remember, after all, is that Lincoln's "stretching" of the Constitution did not cause the American people to lose their liberties. William Dunning might, a generation after the event, as already indicated, characterize Lincoln as a temporary dictator. Such a characterization was, however, far wide of the mark insofar as Lincoln's personal temperament was concerned. His dislike of arbitrary rule, his reasonableness in practice, his willingness to make political compromises, his temperance of military excess—all these were inconsistent with the dictatorial posture.

No dictator would have submitted to the often venomous attacks of much of the Democratic press (the repressions of newspapers referred to earlier were, it should be noted, relatively rare exceptions) or permitted the continuance of his own power to be placed in the electoral balance in the midst of life-and-death conflict. The contrast between the methods of the modern totalitarian dictator and those of the representative product of the sturdy democratic traditions of the pioneer Midwest is self-evident.

It should not be forgotten that war, and above all civil conflict, serves to release the most extreme passions. "War," as the Supreme Court once pointed out, "strips man of his social nature; it demands of him the suppression of those sympathies which claim man for a brother; and accustoms the ear of humanity to hear with indifference, perhaps exultation, 'that thousands have been slain.' "

The measures taken by Lincoln himself were much milder than those urged by the extremists in his party and the country. He himself could urge "the Christian principle of forgiveness on terms of repentance," but the Reconstruction experience gives some indication of what would have happened during the war itself had Lincoln's restraining hand not been present. Most of the nation was ready to go far beyond the President in taking measures to suppress disloyalty. Even so respected a journal as the *Atlantic Monthly* could delete from its pages the description by Nathaniel Hawthorne of an interview with the President because it "lacks *reverence.*"

"The Civil War," says Bruce Catton, "is the thing that makes America different. It was our most tremendous experience." As such, it was bound to have important constitutional, as well as other, effects. The first of these was articulation of the principle laid down in the 1863 *Prize Cases*—the one decision of consequence rendered by the highest bench during the conflict. It arose out of one of the emergency measures taken by Lincoln after the fall of Sumter, namely, his proclamation in April, 1861, of a blockade of all Southern ports. Four ships had been captured by Union naval vessels enforcing the blockade and had been brought into ports to be claimed as prizes. Their owners contended that they had not been lawfully seized, since a blockade was a belligerent act, which could not be proclaimed in the absence of a state of war declared by the Congress.

It has been said that Lincoln's proclamation of a blockade at the outset of the Civil War was a tactical error. According to the usages of international law, a blockade implies a state of belligerency. In its proclamation of neutrality, issued in May, 1861, Great Britain took note of such belligerency, and Earl

Russell, the British Foreign Secretary, was able to state, in reply to the claim that the Queen's proclamation was "precipitate": "It was, on the contrary, your own Government which, in assuming the belligerent right of blockade, recognized the Southern States as belligerents."

Be that as it may, however, it can hardly be denied that the proclamation of a blockade, with the recognition of belligerency implied in it, constitutes an act of war. To the Supreme Court, indeed, it was Lincoln's proclamation of a blockade that constituted the beginning of the Civil War. But could the President thus begin a war without violating what the shipowners claimed to be the "inexorable rule" that the country could be involved in war legally only by declaration of the Congress?

The high Court in the *Prize Cases* avoided a direct answer to this question by stating that the President did not, by his blockade proclamation or any other act, initiate the conflict between the states. In his argument before the Court on behalf of the government, William M. Evarts had urged, "War is, emphatically, a question of actualities." Whenever a situation assumes the proportions and pursues the methods of war, he said, the peace is driven out, and the President may assert the warlike strength of the nation.

Evarts' approach was essentially that followed by the Supreme Court in the *Prize Cases.* The actuality of the situation confronting Lincoln after Sumter was one of war. In the high bench's phrase, "However long may have been its previous conception, it nevertheless sprung forth from the parent brain, a Minerva in the full panoply of *war*." The President did not initiate the war, but he was bound to accept the challenge without waiting for a congressional declaration. Since a state of war actually existed, the President could resort to belligerent measures to deal with it, though there had been no congressional declaration.

The bare holding of the *Prize Cases* was that the President could deal with the situation after Sumter as a war and employ what belligerent measures he deemed necessary without waiting for Congress to declare war. But the implications of the Court's decision are much broader. "It is in vain," Evarts had argued for the government, ". . . to argue that only Congress can declare war." The *Prize Cases* are so important because the Supreme Court accepted this view. War, said the opinion, is: "That state in which a nation prosecutes its right by force." Under such a definition, the President can, in fact (if not in the technical contemplation of the Constitution), initiate a war. The *Prize Cases* constitute a clear rejection of the doctrine that only the Congress can stamp a hostile situation with the character of war and thereby authorize the legal consequences which ensue from a state of war.

Rejection of the rule that only Congress can initiate war has been of tremendous practical significance. If the President could initiate belligerent measures to cope with civil rebellion, why might he not do so to deal with hostile invasion? In such a case, also, the President would plainly be empowered to meet the challenge as war, without waiting for any congressional declaration. It would nonetheless be a war for the fact that it was begun, not by formal declaration, but by unilateral act.

Must the President, however, be limited to the power to resort to belligerent measures only after the first blow has been struck against the nation? Such a limitation could well mean national annihilation in an age in which a potential enemy has at its disposal the absolute power to destroy other nations. A Constitution which did not permit the Commander in Chief to order belligerent acts whenever they are deemed necessary to defend the interests of the nation would be less an instrument intended to endure through the ages than a suicide pact.

The language of the high Court in the *Prize Cases* is broad enough to empower the President to do much more than merely parry a blow already struck against the nation. Properly construed, in truth, it constitutes juristic justification of the many instances in our history (ranging from Jefferson's dispatch of a naval squadron to the Barbary Coast to the 1962 blockade of Cuba) in which the President has ordered belligerent measures abroad without a state of war having been declared by Congress.

The key passage of the *Prize Cases* opinion in this respect asserts that whether the President "has met with such armed hostile resistance, and a civil war of such alarming proportions as will compel him to accord to them the character of belligerents, is a question to be decided by *him.*" The judiciary must be governed by his decisions and acts in the matter. In other words, whether the President has met with a situation which requires him to resort to an act of war to defend the interests of the nation is for him to decide. "He must determine what degree of force the crisis demands." Nor, if he judges the situation to be such as to demand recourse to belligerent action, is he barred from it by the fact that war has not been declared by Congress. On the contrary, a state of war may exist without a declaration, and the President's action in ordering an act of war is itself a clear indication that such a state does exist. In the words of the *Prize Cases* opinion, "The proclamation of blockade is itself official and conclusive evidence to the Court that a state of war existed which demanded and authorized a recourse to such a measure."

In addition to the power to initiate a state of war, the President possesses the authority to wage war. In virtue of his constitutional position as Commander in Chief, he is, in Hamilton's phrase, "the first general and admiral of the confederacy"—the supreme commander of the nation's might. As John Marshall put it in a noted debate in the House of Representatives before his elevation to the high bench, "The President . . . holds and directs the force of the nation. Of consequence, any act to be performed by the force of the nation is to be performed through him."

It was during the Civil War that the full import of the commander-in-chief clause (Article II, section 2) became apparent. As Commander in Chief, Lincoln played whatever part he chose in the direction of military movements and strategy, and even the actual conduct of military operations. He chose the different commanders and at times—not always happily—interfered directly in command matters, as when, early in 1862, he ordered a military advance. It was as Commander in Chief, too, that Lincoln took the measures, discussed earlier, which infringed upon civil liberties, as well as that action of his which gave rise to perhaps the greatest contemporary constitutional controversy: his issuance of the Emancipation Proclamation.

It is difficult for us today, only a hundred years later, even to realize the controversial nature of Lincoln's historic action in decreeing emancipation. "This," writes Andrew McLaughlin, a leading twentieth-century historian, "more than most problems we have discussed, appears to us now as purely academic and as far away as Genghis Khan." For, to us, the indefensible nature of slavery as a moral and historical anachronism is self-evident. To most men a hundred years ago, the situation was altogether different. Even Lord Acton, apostle of liberty though he was later to become, could write soon after Sumter, "It is as impossible to sympathise on religious grounds with the categorical prohibition of slavery as, on political grounds, with the opinions of the abolitionists."

Lincoln himself, it is well known, was far from an extreme abolitionist. Regardless of his personal intense convictions on the moral evil of slavery—that "monstrous injustice" he had called it as early as 1854—he was still a relative moderate when it came to practical measures to eliminate the evil. He conceded that the Federal Government lacked the power to interfere with the peculiar institution in the states, and, in his First Inaugural Address, expressly disclaimed any intention to infringe upon it. As late as March, 1862, Lincoln proposed a scheme for gradual compensated abolition as the proper solution. In August, 1862, he wrote, in his celebrated letter to Horace Greeley, that his paramount object was to save the Union, not to save or destroy slavery: "If I could save the Union without freeing any slave, I would do it; and if I could do it by freeing all the slaves, I would do it; and if I could save it by freeing some and leaving others alone, I would also do that."

Thus Lincoln's view was that if he did anything about slavery, he would do it only because it would help to win the war. But now, in mid-1862, in Bruce Catton's characterization, the machine was stalling, and he had to get it moving again; he had concluded that to do this he would have to call on the emotional power of the antislavery cause. On the first day of 1863, the definitive step was taken. By his own proclamation, issued without express constitutional or statutory authority, Lincoln ordered and declared "that all persons held as slaves" within the states then in rebellion "are, and henceforward shall be free."

By way of parenthetical aside, the issuance of the Emancipation Proclamation also illustrates for constitutional scholars the position of the President vis-à-vis his Cabinet. The story is told that when Lincoln submitted the draft of his proclamation to the Cabinet, he met strong opposition. After a vote, in which the entire Cabinet voted against the issuing of the document, Lincoln is said to have stated the result of the vote as follows: "Seven against: one for. The ayes have it." Though generally considered apocryphal today, the anecdote demonstrates conclusively the complete ascendancy of the President over the members of his Cabinet, who, legally speaking, are merely the instruments by which the policy of their chief is carried out. Men like William H. Seward and Salmon P. Chase, who hoped to dominate the government from their Cabinet posts, overlooked not only the true personality of the President, but also the constitutional realities of their positions.

As already indicated, the Emancipation Proclamation itself was an object of much constitutional controversy. It was attacked on legal grounds both as beyond the scope of federal power and as a usurpation of power by the Executive. If the proclamation is to find constitutional support, it must be in the war powers of the President as Commander in Chief. This was the basis articulated in the proclamation, which declared that it was issued "by virtue of the power in me vested as Commander-in-Chief of the Army and Navy . . . and as a fit and necessary war measure." Lincoln himself was later to concede: "The . . . proclamation has no constitutional or legal justification, except as a military measure."

The President's powers as a military commander include belligerent rights derived from the usages of war as well as the authority to govern occupied territory. As such, he may, as the *Prize Cases* squarely recognized, proclaim a blockade of an enemy's coast or he may, as was first done in the Mexican War, set up military governments in areas conquered by American forces. From this point of view, the decreeing of emancipation may be considered an analogous exercise of the President's war power. A military occupier, the Supreme Court itself affirmed in a case growing out of the military government established in conquered New Orleans, "may do anything necessary to strengthen itself and weaken the enemy." The power to free the enemy's slaves, like the power to take over his other property, is included within the power of military occupation. As Richard Henry Dana (known to his contemporaries more as a leading lawyer than as author of a sea classic) expressed it in an 1865 address, "That an army may free the slaves of an enemy is a settled right of law."

Secretary of State Seward derided the Emancipation Proclamation as one "emancipating slaves where we cannot reach them, and holding them in bondage where we can set them free." But the practical effect of Lincoln's historic act can today scarcely be disputed. In the recent words of a prominent Southerner, "Though the North did not enter the war to free the Negro, it did enter it because he was enslaved." To win the war, however, the Union armies soon realized that they would have to deprive the Southern war effort of the property which supported it. "To save the Union," Bruce Catton pungently points out, "the North had to destroy the Confederacy, and to destroy the Confederacy it had to destroy slavery. The Federal armies got the point and behaved accordingly." Where the Union forces penetrated, slavery went out of existence. The Thirteenth Amendment placed the constitutional seal upon the situation as it actually existed in the areas occupied by the Northern armies and also consigned the question of the Emancipation Proclamation's legality to the realm of purely academic controversy.

From a constitutional point of view, the freeing of the slaves was a measure that must be considered revolutionary in nature. It converted the War Between the States into what one may, paraphrasing Lord Acton, term the second American Revolution. Slavery had been the great lacuna in the rule of freedom and equality upon which the Republic had been based—the living lie in the American heritage. While the institution continued, the gulf between ideals and reality remained so wide as to smack of hypocrisy. A constitutional ideal divided against itself also could not stand.

Now, with Lincoln's proclamation and the Thirteenth Amendment, the picture was completely transformed. The notion that a human being could be relegated to the legal status of mere property was repudiated as constitutional heresy. Thenceforth the principles embodied in the Declaration of Independence and the

Bill of Rights could be translated into actuality. The nation could, in Lincoln's phrase, "Return to the fountain whose waters spring close by the blood of the Revolution."

It is true that mere emancipation could not of itself invest the former slave with complete equality. The Civil War gave the Negro constitutional status similar to that of his former master, but it could not and did not give him the moral status in the sight of the white community that was needed to make his freedom workable. For a century thereafter, indeed, the Negro race was placed in the position of second-class citizens. But a second-class citizen, as the experience in our own day is showing, may hope to become something better. The same can scarcely be true of one considered by society and the law to have only the attributes of a chattel.

The Civil War may be considered as an extraconstitutional appeal from the *Dred Scott* decision. In this sense, the Northern victory resulted in the practical reversal of the doctrine laid down in that case by the highest Court and the establishment of a new rule which was thenceforth to govern the legal status of the Negro.

From a Southern point of view, at the same time, if we look at the Civil War in order to determine its impact upon constitutional doctrine, it may be said to be an attempt to overrule the nationalistic conception of the Constitution which had prevailed since the accession of John Marshall to the Chief Justiceship. Virginian though he was, Marshall's dominant aim, we saw, was to establish a strong nation, endowed with the effective powers needed to enable it to govern a continent. The decisions of the great Chief Justice and his colleagues constructed the edifice of federal supremacy upon so strong a base that it has never since been subjected to successful *legal* attack. The adherents of state sovereignty could hope to prevail only by resorting to methods outside the judicial arena. To render the Constitution workable, it had to incorporate "a coercive principle"—the question being, one of the Framers declared, whether it should be "a coercion of law, or a coercion of arms." With national supremacy so firmly established by the coercion of law, its opponents deemed themselves relegated to the coercion of arms, if their view of the nature of the nation was to gain ascendancy.

Thus regarded, the Civil War was the test of fire for the national system created in 1787. "In the body of our Constitution," Chief Justice Warren has stated, "the Founding Fathers insured that the Government would have the power necessary to govern." The Supreme Court, in the half century that followed, consistently construed the basic document so as to endow the nation with all the necessary authority to enable it to fulfill the high purposes set forth in the Preamble. The defeat of the South placed the imprimatur of arms upon both the intent of the Framers and the Marshall interpretation of federal power.

The conduct of the Civil War itself, it should be noted, furnished ample proof of the soundness of the Marshall conception of strong national power. "The Federal Government," Winston Churchill tells us, "gaining power steadily at the expense of the states, rapidly won unquestioned control over all the forces of the Union. The Southern 'Sovereign States,' on the other hand, were unable even under the stress of war to abandon the principle of decentralisation for which they had been contending." The kind of government Southerners wanted was not, in Bruce Catton's characterization, the kind that could fight and win an extended war; states' rights made an impossible base for total conflict.

The Civil War not only confirmed, it accelerated the trend toward strong national government that has been the underlying theme of our constitutional development. "The South," says James McBride Dabbs, himself a leading Southerner, "with whatever justification, tried in '61 to break the Union. She succeeded only in strengthening what she fought against." Out of the conflict arose a true national government—no longer merely *primus inter pares* but the supreme political organ on the North American continent.

Writing as early as 1861, the celebrated correspondent of the London *Times,* "Bull Run" Russell, contemplating the likelihood of Northern success, concluded: "A strong government must be the logical consequence of victory." That is precisely what did happen. And not only because the Southern defeat spelled the end of the extreme state-rights view as plausible constitutional doctrine. The withdrawal of the Southern bloc from Congress enabled economic federalism (of which they had been the only effective opponents) to be pushed to unprecedented lengths. The program of the Northerners desiring government aid was implemented by the national banking system, the Contract Labor Law, the Homestead Act, the Morrill Act, which granted land for agricultural colleges, subsidies for the transcontinental railroads, and other measures. "On the eve of these enactments," Roy F. Nichols declares, "the United States had been a laissez-faire, individual-enterprise state. It was now transformed into a nation with grand ideas of Federal subsidy, encouragement and protection to corporate enterprise."

Most important of all, however, was the fact that the Northern victory settled the dispute between state and national power which had been much of the substance of American constitutional history. Until the Civil War the advocates of state sovereignty could, despite the uniform case law the other way, continue to assert the temporary contractual nature of the Union. The defeat of the South meant the definitive repudiation of such assertion. In the law itself, this repudiation was marked by the landmark case of *Texas v. White,* decided by the Supreme Court shortly after the Civil War.

In *Texas v. White,* the state of Texas brought an original action to enjoin the payment of certain United States bonds owned by the state before the war and negotiated by the Confederate state government to the defendants. The key issue presented to the high bench was whether Texas was then a state of the Union and, as such, capable of bringing suit. Defendants contended that she was not—that, having seceded and not yet being represented in the Congress, she was still out of the Union. As so presented, the case turned on the question of whether or not Texas had ever left the Union.

According to Chief Justice Chase's opinion for the Supreme Court, that question had to be answered in the negative. As far as the law was concerned, the ordinance of secession by Texas was a nullity. Texas consequently always remained a state within the purview of the Constitution: "When, therefore, Texas became one of the United States, she entered into an indissoluble relation. . . . The act which consummated her admission into the Union was something more than a compact; it was the incorporation of a new member into the political body. And it was final. . . . There was no place for reconsideration, or revocation."

It is all too easy to dismiss *Texas v. White* as only the judicial ratification of the real decision on the validity of secession which had been made at Appomattox Courthouse. To be sure, if the actual outcome of the conflict had been different, the Supreme Court decision could never have been made. But that is true because the constitutional nature of the Union would have been completely altered by military power. On the other hand, as a purely legal decision, under the Constitution as it is written, *Texas v. White* is sound.

It is "self-evident," in Thomas Cooley's words, "that the Union could scarcely have had a valuable existence had it been judicially determined that powers of sovereignty were exclusively in the states." The very language of the organic document refutes the notion that the states do have a sovereign right to secede at will. The Articles of Confederation themselves declared the Union's character to be "perpetual." "And," says Chief Justice Chase, "when these Articles were found to be inadequate to the exigencies of the country, the Constitution was ordained 'to form a more perfect Union.' It is difficult to convey the idea of indissoluble unity more clearly than by these words. What can be indissoluble if a perpetual Union, made more perfect, is not?"

The Constitution is thus a bond of national unity—not a mere federal league dissoluble at the pleasure of any party to it. "The Constitution of the United States," said Justice Joseph P. Bradley in 1871, "established a government, and not a league, compact or partnership. . . . The doctrine so long contended for, that the Federal Union was a mere compact of States, and that the States, if they chose, might annul or disregard the acts of the National legislature, or might secede from the Union at their pleasure, and that the General Government had no power to coerce them into submission to the Constitution, should be regarded as definitely and forever overthrown."

From a legal point of view, then, the nature of the Union is definitely settled. The Union instituted by the men of 1787 is complete, perpetual, and indissoluble. "The Constitution," declares *Texas v. White,* "in all its provisions, looks to an indestructible Union, composed of indestructible States."

VI

CONGRESS OVER CONSTITUTION

THE CONSTITUTIONAL STRUCTURE erected by the Framers had been preserved by "those who . . . gave their lives that that nation might live"—to such an extent, indeed, that it could not be shaken even by the excesses of the Reconstruction period. It is well known that Lincoln's own attitude toward the binding up of the nation's wounds—summed up in classic terms in that Second Inaugural Address which Charles Francis Adams, Jr., characterized "as being for all time the historical keynote of this war"—was not shared by those who held the reins of actual power during Reconstruction. Lincoln's own vision was soon blotted out: "With malice toward None; with charity for all" was replaced by the law of military occupation. "Today," wrote Heinrich Schliemann (later celebrated as the excavator of Troy) on an 1868 visit to the United States, the Southern states "are being treated like a conquered territory. They are under martial law, without political representation, without money, banks, or means of defending themselves."

President Johnson proclaimed the end of the rebellion in April, 1866, and the Supreme Court held that this marked the legal termination of the Civil War. But the radical leaders in the Congress refused to accept the presidential view in the matter and resolved to treat the defeated South more or less in accordance with the "conquered provinces theory" enunciated by Congressman Thaddeus Stevens. After the radicals' victory in the congressional election of 1866, they were able to secure the enactment, over Johnson's veto, of the notorious Reconstruction Act of March, 1867. Under that law, the South was divided into five military districts, each under a general with the necessary troops at his disposal. These generals were to oversee reconstruction in their districts, to suppress disorders, and, if need be, to establish military commissions for the trial and punishment of offenders.

The defenders of the Reconstruction Act sought to justify it by reliance on the constitutional obligation of the United States to guarantee to every state a republican form of government. Such attempted justification was, however, but a patent pretense. As Johnson pungently put it in his veto message, "The purpose and object of the bill—the general intent which pervades it from beginning to end—is to change the entire structure and character of the State governments and to compel them by force to the adoption of organic laws and regulations which they are unwilling to accept if left to themselves."

From a constitutional point of view, nevertheless, it must be conceded that the question of proper enforcement of the guaranty of republican government is one that is solely for the political departments. Such had been the holding of the highest Court itself in the noted 1849 case of *Luther v. Borden.* The Reconstruction experience shows what legally uncontrollable power in the political branches can mean in practice. Since enforcement of the constitutional guaranty is, under *Luther v. Borden,* left to the absolute discretion of the Congress, there is no legal check to restrain that body from converting the republican guaranty clause into a source of tremendous power. In writing about the constitutional provision in question, Madison, in *The Federalist,* had asked "whether it may not become a pretext for alteration in the State governments without the concurrence of the States themselves." The possibility referred to became an actuality after the Civil War.

In *Texas v. White,* discussed at the end of the preceding chapter, the highest Court construed the republican guaranty clause as authorizing Congress to establish and maintain governments in those states which had attempted to secede. But the Congress did not limit itself to insuring to the people of the Southern states the establishment of republican governments responsible to themselves. Instead it assumed complete control over the reconstruction of government in those states. Governments were imposed and retained in power by military force during the entire Reconstruction period; these governments the Congress termed republican in form, though they were instituted against the will of most of the citizens of the states concerned.

There may well have been justification for treating the vanquished South as occupied territory to be ruled by military governments established by the occupying power. There was none for perverting the constitutional form and doing utter violence to the republican guaranty clause. At the same time, from the legal point of view alone, it is plain that the decision in *Luther v. Borden* vested uncontrollable authority in the matter in the Congress. The holding of *Luther v. Borden,* the opinion in *Texas v. White* affirms, can be applied "with even more propriety" to the situation after the Civil War: then, too, "the power to carry into effect the clause of guaranty is . . . a legislative power, and resides in Congress."

Legal issues aside, it can scarcely be gainsaid that the war and postwar periods left a permanent mark on the South which still drastically affects our constitutional development. A Southern writer, James McBride Dabbs, has compared the post-bellum South to a frontier: "First, a physical frontier—not, this time, unbroken forest, but twisted rails, blown bridges, blackened ruins." Second, an unsettled social frontier, in the disordered area of race relations. The violence and disrespect for law that has characterized much of the South has been a normal by-product of frontier conditions.

It should not be forgotten that, in political, as in natural, science, an equivalent of Newton's third law (to every force an equal and opposite reaction) holds sway. The extreme measures taken during Reconstruction were bound to result in a comparable reaction in the opposite direction, when once the Southerners regained control of their own destiny. The sense of white solidarity, the fear of black domination, the attempt to restore a copy of the old racial order—these were natural (even if not ethically justifiable) fruits of the post-bellum period.

This is true even though the full pattern of segregation, based upon Jim Crow laws, did not become established throughout the South until after the turn of the century. As C. Vann Woodward, whose researches have shown the relative recency of *legally enforced* segregation, points out, "although the segregation system is relatively new, it is grounded upon theories and attitudes that are not at all new." The reaction to Reconstruction began before the era of legal segregation, though there were also countervailing efforts at racial accommodation which finally failed in the face of prevailing sentiment. Ultimately, the Reconstruction period ended in an extreme reaction from the aims of the Northern reformers. "In the end," in Woodward's phrase, "it was the will of the defeated, discredited, and, for a time, helpless South that prevailed."

In some ways, the most interesting constitutional lesson of the Reconstruction era is its illustration of the dire consequences that must ensue when the system of checks and balances erected by the Framers gives way to one of uncontrolled supremacy in the legislative department. The men of 1787, with the lesson of the Articles of Confederation before them, were well aware of what congressional primacy in administration, as well as legislation, meant in practice. The experience during the Civil War, with the irresponsible attempts of the congressional Committee on the Conduct of the War to take over the direction of the war effort, furnished a foretaste of what was to come during the postwar period of legislative predominance.

The Reconstruction Congress itself did not rest content with formulating the policy that was to govern the rehabilitation of the defeated states. Instead, fearing lest its repressive policy be frustrated by the other two departments, it sought to curb their powers to such an extent that they would become mere sterile adjuncts of the legislative will. "If the Constitution got in their way," says Woodward of the architects of Reconstruction, "they changed it or ignored it, and they took much the same attitude toward the President and the Supreme Court."

Basic to the plan of the radical congressional leaders in this respect was what Roy F. Nichols has termed the making over of the Executive after their own image. Johnson was to be shorn of the substance of presidential authority and, when that unfortunate remained contumacious, was to be removed by impeachment.

To curb the President, laws were passed limiting his pardoning power and restricting his authority over the armed forces. Then came the Tenure-of-Office Act, which provided that senatorial consent should be necessary for the removal, as well as the appointment, of all civil officers. Johnson had vetoed the law as an encroachment upon his constitutional prerogative (a view which the Supreme Court was to uphold in the leading 1926 *Myers* case); but, as in most other instances, his veto was overridden.

The Tenure-of-Office Act was a virtual sword at the throat of effective presidential power. Without the removal power, which had first been effectively exercised by Andrew Jackson (as seen in Chapter IV), the President could not hope to retain his position as effective administrative chief of the executive establishment. Johnson was, therefore, bound to resist enforcement of the new law if he hoped to preserve more than ceremonial status for the highest office. Despite the Tenure-of-Office Act, Johnson removed his Secretary of War from office, though the Senate had refused its consent. This, in turn, furnished the occasion for the President's impeachment.

The failure of the Senate to vote Johnson guilty (albeit by the slenderest of margins) was of crucial constitutional importance—at least comparable in significance to the like failure to convict Justice Samuel Chase (discussed in Chapter III). If the miscarriage of the Chase impeachment was a vital condition for the development of an independent judiciary, the same may be said of the similar result of the Johnson impeachment insofar as the independence of the executive branch has been concerned.

Had the impeachment of the President on political grounds alone succeeded, it would have ruptured the clear separation intended by the Framers between the executive and legislative departments. "Once set the example," declared Senator Lyman Trumbull, in explaining his vote for Johnson, "of impeaching a President for what, when the excitement of the hour shall have subsided, will be regarded as insufficient cause, and no future President will be safe who happens to differ with a majority of the House and two thirds of the Senate on any measure deemed by them important, particularly if of a political character." Had the Senate voted differently, it might well have established in the American system something very much like the executive dependence on the legislature that prevails in a parliamentary system.

The Johnson impeachment, in addition to its vital impact just referred to, also settled the important, though narrower, question of the reach of the relevant constitutional provision. The Constitution provides for impeachment for "Treason, Bribery, or other high Crimes and Misdemeanors." On its face, this language seems limited to criminal offenses. Johnson's impeachment was, however, based upon a different theory.

The articles of impeachment charged Johnson, not with any indictable offense, but with his failure to carry out certain laws and for his public utterances, especially those attacking the Congress. This, in the argument of the managers of the proceeding, was enough. An impeachable offense, they urged, "may consist of a violation of the Constitution, of law, of an official oath, or of duty, by an act committed or omitted, or, without violating a positive law, by the abuse of discretionary powers from improper motives or for an improper purpose."

Johnson's acquittal represents the definitive rejection of this view, at least so far as the impeachment of executive officers is concerned. Former Justice Benjamin R. Curtis, in his argument in Johnson's defense, stated what may be taken as the prevailing law: "when the Constitution speaks of 'treason, bribery, and other high crimes and misdemeanors,' it refers to, and includes only, high criminal offenses against the United States, made so by some law of the United States existing when the acts complained of were done."

While the Reconstruction Congress was thus seeking (and, in large part, succeeding in its effort) to override the Constitution, that august tribunal, which in our system is endowed with the sacred duty of guarding the organic ark, remained in the state of recession which its *Dred Scott* decision had induced. Unconstitutional though much of the congressional program may have been, the Supreme Court itself was unable so to rule in any of the important cases brought before it during the Reconstruction period itself.

It is true that the high bench did render decision in the 1866 *Milligan* case. The decision there was referred to by Chief Justice Warren, in his 1962 James Madison Lecture, as a "landmark," which "established firmly the principle that when civil courts are open and operating, resort to military tribunals for the prosecution of civilians is impermissible." Yet, vital though *Milligan* has been as the foundation of the wall of separation between the military and civil classes in the community, it had little immediate practical effect.

During the war itself, the Supreme Court had refused to rule on the legality of Vallandigham's arrest. The holding of illegality in the similar *Milligan* fact pattern came over a year after the war was over. Milligan himself may have had the satisfaction of being immortalized in the *Supreme Court Reports;* but that hardly was an adequate substitute for the illegal imprisonments suffered by Copperheads and others while the highest Court declined to come to grips with the constitutionality of military arrests and trials.

The *Milligan* decision itself did not prevent the provision in the Reconstruction Act of 1867 for military rule and trial by military commissions (of the very type which *Milligan* had ruled illegal) in the Southern states. Efforts to prevent the enforcement of the 1867 act, on the ground of its patent unconstitutionality, by injunction suits against the President and the Secretary of War were dismissed by the Supreme Court as not within judicial competence. Then came the case of *Ex parte McCardle,* which, at first, appeared likely to bring the issue of the legality of congressional Reconstruction squarely before the high court.

The *McCardle* case arose out of the arrest under the Reconstruction Act of a Mississippi newspaper editor. Held for a trial by military commission, he petitioned for a writ of *habeas corpus* in the federal circuit court, challenging the validity of the Reconstruction Act's provision which authorized the military detention and trial of civilians. The writ was denied by the circuit court and an appeal was taken to the Supreme Court under a statute authorizing appeals from circuit court decisions in all cases involving detentions in violation of the Constitution or federal laws.

The high bench unanimously decided that it had jurisdiction to hear the appeal. The case was then thoroughly argued upon the merits and was taken under advisement by the Justices. The Court had two years earlier decided against the wartime trial of civilians by military commission in the already discussed *Milligan* case, and it was widely believed that it would seize the occasion presented by the *McCardle* appeal to invalidate the military governments authorized by the Reconstruction Act. The Congress, to avoid this danger, passed a bill repealing the statute authorizing an appeal to the Supreme Court from circuit court judgments in *habeas corpus* cases, and prohibiting the Court's exercise of any jurisdiction on appeals which had been or which might be taken. Though his impeachment trial had already begun, President Johnson did not hesitate to meet the congressional attack on the high tribunal with a strongly worded veto. The bill was repassed over the presidential negative. The *McCardle* case was then reargued on the question of the authority of the Congress to withdraw jurisdiction from the Supreme Court over a case which had already been argued on the merits.

The high Court in its *McCardle* decision unanimously ruled that it no longer had any jurisdiction over the case. The effect of the relevant statute was plain: namely, to withdraw jurisdiction over the appeal. It is quite clear, therefore, the Court concluded, "that this court cannot proceed to pronounce judgement in this case, for it has no longer jurisdiction of the appeal."

The *McCardle* case strikingly demonstrates the fallen state of the Supreme Court in the post-*Dred Scott* period. The statute involved in *McCardle* had as its sole purpose and end the prevention of a decision by the high bench on the constitutionality of the Reconstruction Act. The *McCardle* law has, indeed, been characterized as the only instance in American history in which Congress has rushed to withdraw the appellate jurisdiction of the Supreme Court for the purpose of preventing a particular decision on the constitutionality of a particular law. And the *McCardle* decision itself permitted the Congress to do just that. "Congress," wrote former Justice Curtis (himself the author of the celebrated *Dred Scott* dissent) at the time of *McCardle,* "with the acquiescence of the country, has subdued the Supreme Court."

Yet, if what has just been said demonstrates the clear domination of the Congress in the immediate post-bellum governmental structure, and the diminished role of the judicial department, the constitutional center of gravity was soon once again to shift. And, paradoxically enough, the principal impetus for the shift was provided by that Fourteenth Amendment whose enactment was itself a crucial part of the radical Reconstruction program.

The post-Civil War amendments (ratified in 1865, 1868, and 1870) constituted the first changes in the constitutional text in over sixty years. The Thirteenth Amendment was plainly necessary to resolve the unsatisfactory status of slavery—that "king's cure" for the slavery evil, Lincoln aptly termed it. But mere abolition of slavery was scarcely enough to vest the Negro with anything like the civil status of others in the community. The Fourteenth Amendment was needed to provide for equality of the races in the possession of fundamental civil rights. The Fifteenth Amendment completed the picture by giving the Negro the right of suffrage, which is the primary attribute of effective citizenship.

It is the first section of the Fourteenth Amendment that deals specifically with the question of civil rights. It was intended to have two principal effects. The first was to sweep away the *Dred Scott* decision barring citizenship for the Negro. "All persons born or naturalized in the United States," it reads, ". . . are citizens [both] of the United States and of the State wherein they reside."

In addition, the intent was to make it illegal for the states to deny equal civil rights to those thus made citizens. The Negro was to be given the protection of due process and equality before the law. Hence, the provision that no state was to "deprive any person of life, liberty, or property without due process of law" or to "deny to any person within its jurisdiction the equal protection of the laws." These two clauses—the due process clause and the equal protection clause—of the Fourteenth Amendment were completely to transform the American constitutional system. Much of the stuff of our constitutional law in the century that has followed has, in truth, been in the nature of mere gloss upon those two pregnant provisions.

Not least of the constitutional perversions practiced by the congressional radicals was the manner in which they secured the ratification of the post-bellum amendments—particularly the Fourteenth. In effect, the amendments were steam-rollered through the Southern states (without whose adherence the requisite three-fourths majorities would have been lacking) as part of the price of defeat. The question of how a state could be treated by them as a "conquered province" and still be permitted to perform the supreme function of ratifying an amendment to the fundamental law was one which apparently did not even trouble the radical leaders.

The white South has consistently attacked the Fourteenth and Fifteenth Amendments on the ground that they were force bills. To this, one may quote the query of a prominent Southerner: "One may ask seriously: so what? The South had appealed to force. When it lost this appeal, it had to pay the penalty, not only of military defeat, but also of political reprisals." Without a doubt, the amendments in question were intended to work hardship on the South and to do so without regard to Southern inclinations and desires; that is the normal purpose of terms imposed upon a defeated power.

Nevertheless, imposed by coercion or not, the Fourteenth and Fifteenth Amendments must now clearly be considered a part of the Constitution, for they were declared duly ratified in accordance with the established forms. As the Supreme Court put it in the leading case on the matter, after reciting the circumstances relating to the adoption of the Fourteenth Amendment and the resolution and proclamation of ratification by the Congress and the Secretary of State, "This decision by the political departments of the Government as to the validity of the adoption of the Fourteenth Amendment has been accepted."

One may go further and say that, regardless of the manner of their adoption, the post-bellum amendments have been accepted without question as part of the supreme law of the land for nearly a century by the vast majority of Americans. More than that, their provisions have accorded with the felt need for equal justice among all men. The Declaration of Independence does not, as Lincoln once expressed it, say that "all men are created equal, except Negroes." The Fourteenth and Fifteenth Amendments have by now been built into the conscience of the nation.

Yet, though the framers of the Fourteenth and Fifteenth Amendments intended them to secure to the Negro the full enjoyment of his new freedom, they used words of general, rather than merely particular, application. This has meant that the vital guarantees laid down safeguard all persons in the community—not only those for whose immediate benefit they were intended. The Fourteenth Amendment especially could develop into a great charter for the protection of the rights of property against governmental encroachment. It is, indeed, one of the ironies of American constitutional history that, for the better part of a century, the Fourteenth Amendment was of little practical help to the very race for whose benefit it was enacted, at the very time that it was serving to shield the excesses of expanding capital from governmental restraints.

If, till our own day, due process and equal protection remained mere slogans for the Negro, they became far more for other classes in the community. As will be seen in the next two chapters, the Supreme Court was to utilize the Fourteenth Amendment over and over to safeguard individual property rights, including those of corporations. And, in doing so, the high bench was virtually to arrogate for itself the predominance in the polity that, during the Reconstruction period, had been in the legislative department. This outcome was doubtless the last thing intended by the radical congressional leaders, but the constitutional changes induced by them led directly to that expansion of judicial power, and correlative diminution of legislative authority, that was shortly to characterize the American system.

The adoption of the post-Civil War amendments plainly mark an epoch in the constitutional history of the nation. Like the

Northern victory itself, they constituted the culmination of the nationalistic theory that had first taken root eighty years earlier in Philadelphia.

From the founding of the Republic to the end of the Civil War, it was the states which were the guardians of the civil liberties of their citizens, and they alone could determine the character and extent of such rights. The Bill of Rights, it should be emphasized, was binding upon the Federal Government alone—not the states. So the Supreme Court had held in the 1833 case of *Barron v. Mayor of Baltimore,* and its decision to that effect had never been questioned. As far as the Federal Constitution was concerned, then, the states were free to encroach upon individual rights as they chose, except for the comparatively minor restrictions contained in the contract and ex-post-facto clauses of Article I, section 10.

Now, with the adoption of the post-bellum amendments, particularly the Fourteenth Amendment, all this was changed. The Fourteenth Amendment called upon the national government to protect the citizens of a state against the state itself. Thenceforth, the safeguarding of personal and property rights was to become primarily a federal function. More than that, such safeguarding was, in practice, to be essentially the task of the courts. Hence, the constitutional power shift, that was to occur toward the end of the century, from the legislative to the judicial department.

The Civil War and the post-bellum amendments, as noted above, mark an epochal turning point in American constitutional development. Before Sumter, the great theme in our constitutional history was the nation-state problem. Regardless of the Framers' intent and the law laid down by the Marshall and Taney Courts, nation and states all too often appeared to confront each other as equals, and all was, in Robert G. McCloskey's characterization, overshadowed by the danger that centrifugal forces would tear the nation apart.

Appomattox put an end to this danger. Thenceforth, the Union was, as described in *Texas v. White,* "indestructible" and the supremacy of federal power was insured. The law could now turn from the federal-state problem to the constitutional issues posed by the burgeoning industrialism of the latter part of the nineteenth century. The focus of constitutional concern could be transferred from the protection of federal power, to the safeguarding of individual rights against governmental power, particularly in the economic sphere.

VII

DUE PROCESS DOMINANT

"As a result of the war," declared Lincoln in an 1864 letter, "corporations have been enthroned and an era of corruption in high places will follow." If the letter in question was actually written by the great emancipator (though often quoted, it is considered to be spurious by the Abraham Lincoln Association), he displayed remarkable foresight, for he anticipated, in a nutshell as it were, the outstanding traits of post-Civil War American society. This was particularly true of the Gilded Age of the later years of the century.

The industrial development of the nation had been tremendously accelerated by the need to mobilize all resources to meet the demands of history's first total war. The Civil War, Bruce Catton points out, pushed the North into the industrial age a full generation sooner than would otherwise have been the case. In 1860, the value of manufactured goods had, for the last time, trailed that of agricultural products. By the war's end, the North had become the great industrialized nation that even a Hamilton could but dimly foresee. "The Civil War," states Harold Underwood Faulkner's standard treatise on American economic history, "brought an Industrial Revolution, and it is this development of the Industrial Revolution which was the outstanding feature of American economic life in the half century since 1860."

The postwar industrial expansion brought about a situation for which the earlier era of relative rustic simplicity could furnish no parallel. It transferred masses of population from the land and concentrated them in urban areas; it transformed the relationship of master and servant as it had existed since the colonial period; it shifted wealth and the power that wealth gives from commerce and agriculture to manufacturing and transportation. It altered the whole social and economic fabric.

Headlong industrialization inevitably raised new problems for the law, and the constitutional history of the nation in the half century after Appomattox must largely be written in terms of the reaction of the legal order to the new industrial economy. If, before the Civil War, the major constitutional theme was the nation-state relationship, in the period that followed, the dominant concern became the relationship between government and business. The danger that state sovereignty would unduly impair the power of the nation was replaced by the danger that government would unduly impede business in its destined industrial conquest of a continent.

The key constitutional provision of the new industrial era was that Fourteenth Amendment which, as seen in the preceding chapter, was the most pregnant of the legal changes imposed by the radical Republicans as part of the price of Southern defeat. For it was the due process clause of that amendment that was to serve as the great charter for the protection of the private enterprise that was so transforming the society.

In this connection, it is important to recall the point made in Chapter IV with regard to the crucial role of the corporation in the economic expansion of the nation. This role was especially vital in the post-Civil War period of rapid industrialization. Without effective use of the corporate device, the capital and other resources needed for the industrial metamorphosis that occurred could scarcely have been found.

For the corporation to play the part it did in the economic life of the nation, it was essential that those who were asked to pool their wealth should know that they could do so free from the risk of governmental infringement. Such assurance was provided by the concept of due process as it was developed in the latter part of the nineteenth century.

Two important stages in the interpretation of the Fourteenth Amendment were necessary for the development just referred to. The first was the inclusion of corporations within the category of "persons" protected by the amendment. The second was the judicial construction of the due process clause as a limitation of substance, as well as one of procedure, upon government.

As indicated in the last chapter, the primary intent of the draftsmen of the Fourteenth Amendment was to secure to the Negro the full enjoyment of his new freedom. But the language employed by them was of general application. Thus, the new constitutional safeguards were expressly made applicable to "any person."

Legal historians have differed on whether the framers of the Fourteenth Amendment did intend to include corporations in the "persons" protected by its provisions. A decade and a half after the adoption of the amendment, Roscoe Conkling, who had been a member of the joint congressional committee which had done the actual drafting, stated, in argument before the highest Court, that he and his colleagues had deliberately used the word "person" in order to include corporations. "At the time the Fourteenth Amendment was ratified," he averred, ". . . individuals and stock companies were appealing for congressional and administrative protection against invidious and discriminating State and local taxes." The clear implication was that the joint committee had taken cognizance of such appeals and had drafted its text to extend the constitutional protection to corporations.

Commentators on the matter have questioned whether the framers of the Fourteenth Amendment did have the conscious intent to protect corporations which Conkling ascribed to them. From a purely historical point of view, indeed, it definitely appears that Conkling, influenced no doubt by the advocate's zeal, overstated his case. Yet, even if his argument on the real intent of the draftsmen was correct, that alone would not justify the inclusion of corporations within the word "person." After all, what was adopted was the Fourteenth Amendment and not what Roscoe Conkling or the other members of the drafting committee thought about it.

What is clear is that the Supreme Court has consistently assumed that corporations do come within the class of "persons" protected by the Fourteenth Amendment. In the 1886 case of *Santa Clara County v. Southern Pacific Railroad,* less than two decades after the amendment itself had been ratified, the question of whether corporations were "persons" within its meaning was extensively briefed by counsel. At the beginning of oral argument in the case, however, Chief Justice Morrison R. Waite tersely announced: "The court does not wish to hear argument on the question whether the provision in the Fourteenth Amendment to the Constitution, which forbids a State to deny to any person within its jurisdiction the equal protection of the laws, applies to these corporations. We are all of the opinion that it does."

The Court in the *Santa Clara* case was apparently so sure of its ground that it wrote no opinion on the point. Be that as it may, however, the Waite pronouncement definitively settled the law on the matter. In the more recent words of Justice Douglas, "It has been implicit in all of our decisions since 1886 that a corporation is a 'person' within the meaning of the . . . Fourteenth Amendment." Countless cases since *Santa Clara* have proceeded upon the assumption that the Fourteenth Amendment assures corporations, as well as individuals, both due process and the equal protection of the laws.

As already stated, the Conkling argument on the real intent of the framers of the Fourteenth Amendment is not as relevant as the words used by them. Even if it be true that they were immediately concerned only with protection of the Negro, that is not as important as the general language written into their work. A constitutional provision should not be restricted in its application because designed originally to prevent an existing wrong. The wrongs inflicted upon the Negro may have been the direct cause of the Fourteenth Amendment, but its framers deliberately used language broad enough to insure that comparable wrongs might not be inflicted upon any person in the United States. All persons, not merely the enfranchised race, were guaranteed due process and the equal protection of the laws.

It should be emphasized that, as far as the law is concerned, a corporation has always been considered a "person"—albeit only an artificial person created by law. If corporate "persons" were to be excluded from the new constitutional protections, it is difficult to see why only the generic term "person" was employed.

The judicial recognition of corporations as persons entitled to the protection of the Fourteenth Amendment may be explained as a merger of legal and economic theories. The end of the Civil War, as pointed out above, saw a vast expansion in the role of the corporation in the American economy. It had, indeed, become clear, even before the great conflict, that the corporate device was an indispensable adjunct of the nation's growth. Realization of the relationship between the corporation and economic development had already led to decisions of the highest bench (notably *Bank of Augusta v. Earle,* discussed in Chapter IV) favorable to the corporate personality.

It was natural, bearing in mind the tremendous economic expansion of the second half of the nineteenth century, that those entities deemed indispensable to such growth would find ever-increasing favor with the courts. When the ultimate protection of person and property was, by the Fourteenth Amendment, transferred from the states to the nation, the judicial trend in favor of the corporation also became a national one. The role of the corporate person in the post-Civil War economic development made the use of the Fourteenth Amendment to safeguard such persons well-nigh inevitable, whatever may have been the subjective goals of the framers.

If corporations had not been included by the courts within the safeguards of the Fourteenth Amendment, that provision could hardly have developed into the basic charter of the new American economy. Nor could such charter have fostered the galloping industrialism of the post-Civil War period if the due process guaranteed by the amendment had been confined to its literal import of *proper procedure*. It was the judicial importation of a substantive side into due process that made it of such significance as a restriction upon governmental power.

Before the adoption of the Fourteenth Amendment, the term "due process" (which was contained in the Fifth Amendment, as well as many state constitutions) was deemed to relate only to the mode of proceeding which must be pursued by governmental agencies. Under such construction, the due process clause is limited to a guaranty of procedural fairness. From the beginning, it is true, a broader conception of due process had been urged. Though the broader view was, prior to the Civil War, adopted by some state courts (notably the New York Court of Appeals), it found little place in the jurisprudence of the nation's highest bench.

If it was the Fourteenth Amendment, with its prohibitions upon the states, that converted due process into a cornerstone of American constitutionalism, that was true because such development was well-nigh inevitable if the Constitution was to serve as a substantial safeguard for property rights. It should not be forgotten that governmental action dealing with business and economic matters touches no particularized prohibition of the Constitution unless it be the due process clause. If it was to remain free of the latter guaranty, the need to give private enterprise the scope it required in the post-Civil War period could scarcely have been met.

It should not, however, be thought that the development by the Supreme Court of due process as a substantive restraint upon government was one that occurred immediately upon the ratification of the Fourteenth Amendment. On the contrary, the first high-bench decisions under the amendment manifested a most restrictive attitude toward its due process clause. In the earliest cases, the Court appeared unwilling to attribute more than a procedural content to the due process requirement.

The first case in the Supreme Court involving the Fourteenth Amendment was the now celebrated *Slaughter House Cases* (1873). In this case, the Court adopted the limited view that the amendment was intended only to protect the Negro in his newly acquired freedom. That being the case, the due process clause was all but irrelevant in considering the constitutionality of a Louisiana law which conferred upon one corporation the exclusive right to slaughter livestock in New Orleans. Referring to the due process clause, the *Slaughter House* Court declared categorically "that under no construction of that provision that we have ever seen, or any that we deem admissible, can the restraint imposed by the state of Louisiana upon the exercise of their trade by the butchers of New Orleans be held to be a deprivation of property within the meaning of that provision." Under this interpretation, with the due process clause held inapplicable to such a case, the states were left almost as free to regulate the rights of property as they had been before the Civil War.

It is, nevertheless, erroneous to assume that the entire Supreme Court, in the period immediately following the adoption of the Fourteenth Amendment, was in favor of the restrictive interpretation of due process just discussed. On the contrary, starting with the *Slaughter House Cases,* there was a substantial minority which urged a broader view. In *Slaughter House* itself, four Justices strongly disputed the Court's casual dismissal of the due process clause. Foremost among them were Justices Stephen J. Field and Joseph P. Bradley, who delivered vigorous dissents urging the pertinency of due process to the monopoly law there at issue. In their view, the Fourteenth Amendment "was intended to give practical effect to the declaration of 1776 of inalienable rights, rights which are the gift of the Creator; which the law does not confer, but only recognizes."

From the rights guaranteed in the Declaration of Independence to substantive due process was a natural transition in the Field-Bradley approach. As they put it, "Rights to life, liberty, and the pursuit of happiness are equivalent to the rights of life, liberty, and property. These are the fundamental rights which can only be taken away by due process of law." A law like the one at issue in *Slaughter House,* in the dissenting view, did violate due process: "In my view, a law which prohibits a large class of citizens from adopting a lawful employment, or from following a lawful employment previously adopted, does deprive them of liberty as well as property, without due process of law."

A federal judge who came to the bar in 1883 has described the state of high-bench jurisprudence at that time with regard to the matter under discussion. "When this generation of mine opened the reports," he tells us, "the chill of the Slaughter House decision was on the bar . . . the still continuing dissents of Judge Field seemed most unorthodox. The remark in another judgment, that due process was usually what the state ordained, seemed to clinch the matter."

But the law on the subject was soon to be altered. In Justice Frankfurter's words, "As the new protection of the Fourteenth Amendment was persistently invoked by counsel against the growing efforts of the states to regulate economic enterprise, the rejected dissents of Mr. Justice Field gradually established themselves as the views of the Court."

The first indications of the change to the Field-Bradley approach came while its authors were still formally on the minority in the high tribunal. A year after the *Slaughter House* decision, the Court majority conceded that a state statute which arbitrarily deprived a person of property would present a "grave" due-process question, though it held that the law at issue was not such a law. This intimation, by way of *obiter dictum,* that due process might have a substantive aspect, was to be confirmed a decade later in cases involving railroad regulation.

The starting point for the judicial development in the railroad field was the famous 1877 *Granger Cases.* In these decisions, the highest Court upheld the power of the states to regulate the rates of railroads and other businesses affected with a public interest—a holding, never since departed from, which has served as the basis upon which governmental regulation in this country has essentially rested. The Court in the *Granger Cases* did not, however, limit itself to this fundamental holding. Instead, over the vigorous dissent of Justice Field who insisted that the due process clause would bar such a result, it also ruled that the legislative judgment in the fixing of rates was not subject to any judicial review. "For protection against abuses by Legislatures," the Court declared, "the people must resort to the polls, not to the courts."

The extreme *Granger* approach, leaving regulated companies defenseless against even the most arbitrary state action in the rate-fixing field, was soon abandoned. Chief Justice Waite, himself the author of the *Granger* opinions, was to state, less than a decade later, that the power to regulate is not the power to confiscate. In an 1886 case, he warned that, "Under the pretense of regulating fares and freights, the state cannot require a railroad corporation to carry persons or property without reward; neither can it do that which in law amounts to a taking of private property for public use without just compensation, or without due process of law."

The Waite dictum just quoted, which intimates that the regulatory power of the states is subject to substantive judicial control based upon the due process clause, was applied by the Supreme Court itself a few years later in nullifying a state law providing for the fixing of railroad rates. According to the Court there, "The question of the reasonableness of a rate of charge for transportation by a railroad company, involving, as it does, the element of reasonableness both as regards the company and as regards the public, is eminently a question for judicial investigation, requiring due process of law."

Ever since, it has been recognized that the due process clause permits the courts to review the substance of rate-fixing legislation and administrative action taken thereunder—at least to determine whether particular rates are set so low as to be confiscatory.

By the 1890's, the Supreme Court was ready to transform the Field-Bradley conception of due process into the law of the land. What had become the rule in railroad rate cases was to become the general rule in cases involving applications of the due process clause.

Definite adoption by the highest Court of the Field-Bradley view may be dated from the 1897 case of *Allgeyer v. Louisiana,* where, in Justice Frankfurter's words, "Mr. Justice Peckham wrote Mr. Justice Field's dissents into the opinions of the Court." In *Allgeyer,* for the first time, a state law was set aside on the ground that it infringed upon the "liberty" guaranteed by the due process clause. The statute in question prohibited an individual from contracting with an out-of-state marine insurance company for the insurance of property within the state. Such law, it was held, "deprives the defendants of their liberty without due process of law."

The "liberty" referred to in the organic provision, said Justice Rufus W. Peckham's opinion, embraces the rights of property, including that to pursue any lawful calling: "In the privilege of pursuing an ordinary calling or trade, and of acquiring, holding, and selling property, must be embraced the right to make all proper contracts in relation thereto." A state law which takes from its citizens the right to contract outside the state for insurance on their property deprives them of their "liberty" without due process.

Between the dictum of the *Granger Cases,* that for protection against legislative abuses "the people must resort to the polls, not to the courts," and *Allgeyer v. Louisiana* and its progeny lies the history of the emergence of modern large-scale industry, of the consequent public efforts at control of business, and of judicial review of such regulation. Thenceforth, all governmental action—whether federal or state—would have to run the gantlet of substantive due process; the substantive as well as the procedural aspect of such action would be subject to the scrutiny of the highest bench.

While the Fourteenth Amendment was thus being developed as the principal legal safeguard of property rights, what was the constitutional position of the Negro, for whose benefit the post-Civil War amendments had primarily been intended?

An answer to this question must recognize that, as a practical matter, the amendments in question were of little value to the Negro until well after the period of time now under discussion. It is true that the Thirteenth Amendment did put the constitutional stamp on the demise of slavery and that the Fifteenth Amendment invalidated all state laws expressly limiting the franchise at general elections to whites. But these amendments did not prevent the South from keeping the former slave in a state of economic subjection. Nor did they automatically give the Negro the ballot. Instead, resort was had to devices like literacy tests and white primaries to avoid the intent of the Fifteenth Amendment. The practical situation in this respect was neatly summed up in a remark made to James Bryce by a leading Southern politician of the 1880's: "We like the Negro, and we treat him well. We mean to continue doing so. But we vote him."

Even worse was the 1896 Supreme Court decision in *Plessy v. Ferguson.* At issue there was the claim that a Louisiana statute requiring separate railroad accommodations for Negro and white passengers violated the Fourteenth Amendment's requirement of equal protection of the laws. The high Court rejected the contention and held, on the contrary, that mere segregation in transportation did not violate the equal protection clause. The Court rejected "the assumption that the enforced separation of the two races stamps the colored race with a badge of inferiority." Under the Supreme Court's doctrine, so long as laws requiring segregation did not establish unequal facilities for the Negro, he was not denied the equal protection of the laws. As the Court has more recently explained it, "Under that doctrine, equality of treatment is accorded when the races are provided substantially equal facilities, even though these facilities be separate."

Plessy v. Ferguson gave the lie to the American ideal, so eloquently stated by Justice John Marshall Harlan in dissent there: "Our Constitution is color-blind, and neither knows nor tolerates classes among citizens." Upon *Plessy* was built the whole structure of segregation that has been at the heart of the Southern system of racial discrimination.

The *Plessy* ruling was based on the assertion that segregation as such does not mean discrimination; if the Negro felt discriminated against, said the Court, it was "not by reason of anything found in the act, but solely because the colored race chooses to put that construction upon it." To anyone familiar with the techniques of racial discrimination, this view is completely out of line with reality. The device of holding a group of people separate—whether by confinement of Jews to the ghetto, by exclusion of untouchables from the temple, or by segregation of the Negro—is a basic tool of discrimination. "The thin disguise of 'equal' accommodations for passengers in railroad coaches," movingly declared the Harlan dissent, "will not mislead anyone, nor atone for the wrong this day done."

Yet it was to be precisely the requirement of equality of treatment articulated in the *Plessy* opinion that was half a century later to provide the opening wedge for the ultimate overruling of the *Plessy* holding itself. But the judicial emphasis on the requirement of equality was still a long way off when *Plessy* was decided. As far as achievement of the main purpose of its framers was concerned, one must conclude that the Fourteenth Amendment was, at the turn of the century at least, of almost no practical effect.

Before we discuss the manner in which the concept of substantive due process was applied by the Supreme Court during the first part of the present century, a word should be said about the constitutional aspect of the imperial interlude that arose out of the Spanish-American War.

In the broadest sense of extension of territorial dominion, it may be true that imperialism has, from the beginning, been a prominent feature of the American Republic. The Constitution plainly contemplates the expansion of the nation's territory and the Supreme Court recognized at an early date the power of the Federal Government to acquire territory in any mode recognized in international law. Our history, it may be said, has more than once seen the assertion of the force of the nation for territorial conquest. To the claim that the Mexican War was not a war of aggression, Lincoln once replied: "The United States is like the farmer who insisted, 'I ain't greedy 'bout land, I only want what jines mine.' "

Even if the expansion of the Republic from the Atlantic seaboard to continental extent was thus based, at least in large part, upon conquest, it must be conceded that it did, in the main, reject an essential feature of an imperial system—namely, that of conquest as the determining factor in the status of newly acquired territory. Ever since the Northwest Ordinance of 1787, the governing principle had been that no area acquired should be permanently held in a territorial status. The Constitution, as Chief Justice Taney once put it, may authorize the acquisition of territory; but such territory "is acquired to become a State, and not to be held as a colony."

The situation was completely changed by the war with Spain. As a result of that conflict, in Bryce's acute characterization. "The Americans drifted into dominion, and were amazed to find whither they had drifted." For the first time, the United States acquired overseas territories inhabited by peoples diverse in blood, speech, and customs from its own people. The new territories were not intended for statehood and they were treated differently from the way prior territorial acquisitions had been treated.

The acquisitions from Spain posed in acute form the problem of the relationship between conquest and the Constitution. Soon after the Spanish war ended, the question of whether government in the new territories was subject to those constitutional limitations which apply in the continental United States came before the Supreme Court. The Court dealt with that question in a series of 1901 decisions that have come to be known as the *Insular Cases*.

The *Insular Cases* arose out of the statute providing for a government for conquered Puerto Rico. Among that law's provisions were revenue sections, including one requiring certain customs duties to be paid upon goods imported into the United States from that island. It was contended that such a provision was invalid, since Puerto Rico had become a part of the United States within the requirement of Article I, section 8, that "all duties, imposts, and excises shall be uniform throughout the United States." This, in turn, said the high Court, posed the broader question of whether the provisions "of the Constitution extend of their own force to our newly acquired territories."

According to the *Insular Cases,* whether the Constitution follows the flag (as the problem was popularly expressed at the time) depends, in the particular case, upon the type of territory that is involved. The Court drew a distinction between so-called "incorporated" and "unincorporated" territories. The former are those territories which the Congress has incorporated into and made an integral part of the United States. Without express provision by the Congress, territory acquired by the nation remains unincorporated.

Applying the distinction between incorporated and unincorporated territories to Puerto Rico, the Supreme Court found that that island belonged to the latter category: "whilst in an international sense Porto Rico was not a foreign country, since it was subject to the sovereignty of and was owned by the United States, it was foreign to the United States in a domestic sense, because the island had not been incorporated into the United States, but was merely appurtenant thereto as a possession."

Under the *Insular Cases,* the applicability of constitutional limitations to a given territory depends upon whether it is incorporated or unincorporated. In the former, all the constitutional rights and privileges must be accorded, with the exception of those that are manifestly applicable only within the states. But the same is not true in unincorporated territories. In them, a constitutional provision like that governing duties and imposts does not restrict governmental authority.

The *Insular Cases* are not based upon the proposition that the restrictions of the Constitution are never operative outside the continental limits and incorporated territories of the United States. The *Insular Cases* held only that not every provision of the basic document must always be deemed automatically applicable to American governmental action in every part of the world. But they recognized that not all constitutional requirements must stand upon the same footing in this regard. "To sustain the judgment in the case under consideration," declares the opinion of the Court in the principal *Insular* case, "it by no means becomes necessary to show that none of the articles of the Constitution apply to the Island of Porto Rico. There is a clear distinction between such prohibitions as go to the very root of the power of Congress to act at all, irrespective of time or place, and such as are operative only 'throughout the United States' or among the several States."

There is, in other words, a distinction between those constitutional restrictions which are of so fundamental a nature that they are the basis of all free government and other restrictions.

The former alone are an absolute denial of governmental authority under any circumstances or conditions.

The *Insular Cases* may have been the occasion for Mr. Dooley's celebrated remark that, whether or not the Constitution followed the flag, "th' supreme coort follows th' illiction returns." But their holding has remained the basic principle in dealing with the relationship of the Constitution to overseas territories. It was to be of particular pertinence in a later age when the United States was to become a leader of the international community. What the Supreme Court said in those cases with regard to the government provided in territories acquired as a result of the Spanish war was to apply as well to the military governments set up in conquered territory almost half a century later.

In this respect, the Constitution is consistent with the laws of war and international practice in vesting in the nation acting overseas more power than is normally entrusted to those in governmental authority in the American system. At the same time, even the military governor is bound by those restrictions upon government which are deemed fundamental. Even conquest does not remove the constitutional limitations safeguarding essential rights and liberties. Wherever the American government functions, its acts may not be inconsistent with the fundamental principles without which our scheme of ordered liberty could not exist.

VIII

JUDICIAL SUPREMACY AND LAISSEZ FAIRE

"NO FEATURE in the Government of the United States," reads an oft-cited passage by Bryce, "has awakened so much curiosity in the European mind, caused so much discussion, received so much admiration, and been more frequently misunderstood, than the duties assigned to the Supreme Court and the functions which it discharges in guarding the ark of the Constitution."

The most conspicuous aspect of the American system, indeed, has been the power of the Supreme Court to invalidate acts of the duly elected representatives of the people. To outside observers, the power thus exercised by American judges smacks more of political, than judicial, power. To them, the Supreme Court has appeared virtually to exercise the functions of what an English writer termed "a third chamber in the United States" —and, if anything, a chamber superior to the two houses of Congress, for it possesses an absolute veto over the laws enacted by them. Significantly, the leading French study of review of the constitutionality of laws by the United States Supreme Court is entitled *Government by Judiciary.*

The doctrine of judicial supremacy did not, however, come

into being full grown with the establishment of the Republic. Although the doctrine was first enunciated in *Marbury v. Madison* in 1803 (as seen in Chapter III), through the first century under the Constitution most of the important questions of national governmental power were settled in the White House and on the floors of Congress. "The fact of the matter," Corwin tells us, "is that judicial review did not become an important factor of national legislative power till about 1890 and . . . this is so even as to state legislative power."

The augmentation of the high tribunal's role was a direct outgrowth of the development of substantive due process (discussed in the preceding chapter), and the manner in which it was used by the Justices as a restraint upon governmental interventions in the economic sphere.

How the Supreme Court would use substantive due process to protect corporate enterprise from governmental restraints was foreshadowed by the 1895 decision in the crucial *Income-Tax Case*. The majority there ruled invalid the federal income-tax law of 1894, even though a similar statute had previously been upheld. The high-bench decision can be explained less in purely legal terms than in terms of the personal antipathies of the Justices who made up the majority of the Court. Counsel opposing the statute at issue depicted the income tax as "a doctrine worthy of a Jacobin Club," the "new doctrine of this army of 60,000,000—this triumphant and tyrannical majority—who want to punish men who are rich and confiscate their property."

Such an attack upon the income tax (though, technically speaking, irrelevant to the case) found a receptive ear in the Court majority. "The present assault upon capital," declares Justice Field, "is but the beginning. It will be but the stepping-stone to others, larger and more sweeping, till our political contests will become a war of the poor against the rich; a war constantly growing in intensity and bitterness." If the Court were to sanction the income-tax law, "it will mark the hour when the sure decadence of our present government will commence." And this, it should be noted, was said about a law that levied a tax of 2 per cent on incomes above $4,000!

The *Income-Tax* decision provoked a veritable storm of controversy, which was not assuaged until the adoption, in 1913, of the Sixteenth Amendment. For our purposes, the important thing about the case is the indication it gives of the Supreme Court's mentality with regard to governmental "assaults upon capital." For it was judges, imbued with the doctrine articulated in the *Income-Tax* opinion, who now had at their disposal the newly fashioned tool of substantive due process.

Due process as a substantive restraint is essentially a prohibition against arbitrary governmental action. This was the view first urged in dissent by Justices Field and Bradley, the original exponents of substantive due process on the highest Court. When the Field-Bradley concept of due process came to prevail in the high bench, the test of arbitrariness was also adopted by the Court. "The Fourteenth Amendment," said Justice Field, in 1885, this time speaking for all the Justices, "undoubtedly intended . . . that there should be no arbitrary deprivation of life or liberty, or arbitrary spoliation of property." Similar statements may be found in most other cases on the subject toward the end of the last century. Arbitrary power, as the Court itself neatly phrased it, is not due process of law.

Arbitrary action, in the sense in which that term was used in the jurisprudence of the Supreme Court, means action that is willful and unreasonable—depending on the will alone and not done according to reason or judgment. Under this formula, arbitrary action is synonymous with unreasonable action and due process becomes a test of reasonableness.

The reasonableness test received its classic enunciation in the 1905 case of *Lochner v. New York,* where the constitutionality of a state regulatory statute furnished the issue. According to the high Court, the question to be determined in cases involving challenges to legislation on due process grounds is: "Is this a fair, reasonable and appropriate exercise of the police power of the State, or is it an unreasonable, unnecessary and arbitrary interference with the right of the individual?"

To say that due process is to be employed as a rule of reason does not, however, answer the crucial question of how the reasonableness test itself is to be applied in specific cases. More particularly, whose conception of reasonableness with regard to legislation is to control—that of the legislator or that of the judge?

In its opinion in *Lochner v. New York,* the Supreme Court indicated that the reasonableness of a challenged statute, under the due process clause, must be determined as an objective fact by the judge upon his own independent judgment. In *Lochner* the statute at issue was one prescribing maximum hours for bakers. In holding the state law invalid, the Court substituted its judgment for that of the legislature and decided for itself that the statute was not reasonably related to any of the social ends for which governmental power might validly be exercised.

In its opinion, the *Lochner* Court strongly denied that it was substituting its judgment for that of the legislature. Despite such disclaimer, substitution of the judicial for the legislative judgment was the precise thing which did occur in *Lochner.* "This case," asserted the celebrated dissent of Justice Holmes, "is decided upon an economic theory which a large part of the country does not entertain." It was because the *Lochner* Court disagreed with the economic theory upon which the state legislature had acted that it struck down the statute at issue as unreasonable.

Though the Court, even in the heyday of the *Lochner* approach, continually asserted that it was not, like the legislature itself, concerned with the wisdom and policy of legislation, the manner in which it actually acted belied its assertion. And there were times when the true situation was acknowledged by members of the high bench themselves. "But plainly . . . ," avowed Justice James C. McReynolds in an important case, "this Court must have regard to the wisdom of the enactment. At least, we must inquire concerning its purpose and decide whether . . . the end is legitimate and the means appropriate." Justice Harlan on one occasion was even more candid. "I want to say to you young gentlemen," he declared in a lecture to law students, "that if we don't like an act of Congress, we don't have much trouble to find grounds for declaring it unconstitutional."

Under *Lochner,* it was the duty of each individual Justice to determine for himself the objective reasonableness of challenged legislation. Though expressing formal compliance with the principle that any reasonable doubts must be resolved in favor of the constitutionality of legislation, the high bench went on to ask: But whose doubts and by whom resolved? And it went on to answer that it was for the conscience of each individual judge to resolve these matters. As Justice George Sutherland once expressed it, "The oath which he takes as a judge is not a composite oath, but an individual one. And in passing upon the validity of a statute, he discharges a duty imposed upon *him,* which cannot be consummated justly by an automatic acceptance of the views of others which have neither convinced, nor created a reasonable doubt in his mind." The judge cannot subordinate his own personal convictions in determining the validity of a law; indeed, for him to attempt to do so, was for him to lose "faith with his oath [and] his judicial and moral independence."

Nor, it should be noted, was judicial utilization of the *Lochner* approach to substantive due process mere control in the abstract of the wisdom of state legislation. Court control was directed to a particular purpose, namely, the invalidation of state legislation that conflicted with the doctrine of laissez faire which dominated thinking in this country at the turn of the century. What Justice Frankfurter has termed "the shibboleths of a pre-machine age . . . were reflected in juridical assumptions that survived the facts on which they were based. . . . Basic human rights expressed by the constitutional conception of 'liberty' were equated with theories of *laissez-faire*."

The result was that the Fourteenth Amendment became the rallying point for judicial resistance to the efforts of the states to control the excesses and relieve the oppressions of a rising industrial economy. "The paternal theory of government," declared Justice David J. Brewer, one of the principal architects of the post-1890 doctrine of due process, "is to me odious. The utmost possible liberty to the individual, and the fullest possible protection to him and his property, is both the limitation and duty of government." To a court which adopted the Brewer philosophy, the "liberty" protected by the Fourteenth Amendment became synonymous with governmental hands-off in the field of private economic relations. Any legislative encroachment upon the existing economic order became suspect as infected with unconstitutionality. "For years," the highest bench itself stated in 1952, "the Court struck down social legislation when a particular law did not fit the notions of a majority of Justices as to legislation appropriate for a free enterprise system."

The *Lochner* opinion itself set a pattern, both as to doctrine and method, which prevailed for a generation. Not that the pattern was always adhered to; but it did constitute the prevailing current in high Court jurisprudence.

In the generation following *Lochner,* the due process clause was used by the Supreme Court to invalidate a whole host of legislation, particularly laws seeking to regulate economic abuses. In Justice Robert H. Jackson's apt phrase, after *Lochner,* it was a fortunate and relatively innocuous piece of reform legislation that did not run afoul of due process.

The impact of the judicial veto under *Lochner* is perhaps best seen from statistics: in the period between 1890 and 1937, the Supreme Court held invalid 55 federal and 228 state statutes. In truth, Justice Frankfurter informs us, had not the *Lochner* current been altered and "Had not Mr. Justice Holmes' awareness of the impermanence of legislation as against the permanence of the Constitution gradually prevailed, there might indeed have been 'hardly any limit but the sky' to the embodiment of 'our economic or moral beliefs' in that Amendment's 'prohibitions.' "

In no way did the doctrine of substantive due process which prevailed under the *Lochner* approach affect the society more than in its impact upon governmental power to protect the worker from the abuses inherent in industrialism. Such abuses led to legislative attempts to safeguard labor by laying down minimum standards governing the conditions of employment. These laws could not, however, successfully run the gantlet of the new constitutional doctrine. Governmental regulation of the relations between capital and labor was deemed a violation of the liberty of contract that was, until our own day, considered the basic part of the liberty safeguarded by the due process clause.

In a series of decisions rendered during the early part of this century, the Supreme Court rigorously applied the *Lochner* approach and the freedom-of-contract formula derived from it to invalidate statutes regulating the hours of labor, guaranteeing minimum wages, barring so-called "yellow-dog contracts" (making it a condition of employment that the worker will not join a union), or restraining the granting of injunctions in labor disputes.

It is difficult for us today to understand the decisions of half a century ago, which so strictly employed the freedom-of-contract doctrine in order to strike down laws regulating the relations between employer and employee. Living in an age of pervasive regulation designed to insure minimum standards and fair dealing for workers, it is all too natural for us to treat the cases which upheld the right to contract above all else as mere aberrations in the law.

The basic question, affirmed the Supreme Court in *Lochner,* is "which of two powers or rights shall prevail,—the power of the state to legislate or the right of the individual to liberty of person and freedom of contract." A society controlled by regulation from cradle to grave may look back with nostalgia, but scarcely with understanding, upon an era which rigorously opted in favor of the latter right.

Yet, though we now find it hard to comprehend a system grounded upon all but inexorable adherence to freedom of contract, we must, if we are to obtain a true picture of the developing law on the subject under discussion, at least appreciate the extent to which such freedom dominated thought and writing at the turn of the century. A noted English observer, Sir Henry Maine, giving his impression of the American system at that time, could state, "It all reposes on the sacredness of contract and the stability of private property, the first the implement, and the last the reward, of success in the universal competition."

Maine himself had all but crowned the position of freedom of contract in the society of the post-Civil War period by his celebrated generalization of the progress from status to contract. In as famous an epigram as appears in legal literature, Maine summarized the course of legal progress: "we may say that the movement of the progressive societies has hitherto been a movement from *Status to Contract*."

Legal progress, in other words, is a movement from subjection to freedom—and the instrument of such freedom is the right of contract.

This theory of the course of legal development fitted in so well with the laissez-faire political and economic philosophy of the time that it soon got complete possession of the field. It was taken for gospel that law was moving and must move in the direction of free contract. It came to be assumed that any limitation on abstract freedom of contract was a step backward and hence arbitrary and unreasonable. To judges imbued with a genuine faith in the progress from status to contract, there was the strongest presumption against any and all restrictions on the freest possible bargaining. Hence, it seemed to them that the constitutional requirement of substantive due process was violated by legislative attempts to restrict the contractual powers of free men by enacting that men of full age and sound mind in particular callings should not be able to make agreements which other men might make freely.

A half century later, we may assert that, in the labor field, the notion of equality between contracting parties, upon which freedom of contract must be based, is wholly out of line with the facts of a modern industrial society—that, in the words of Justice Harlan F. Stone, "There is grim irony in speaking of the freedom of contract of those who, because of their economic necessities, give their services for less than is needful to keep body and soul together."

To the judges of half a century ago, however, the contrary was true. "In all such particulars," declared the Supreme Court in 1908, "the employer and the employee have equality of right, and any legislation that disturbs that equality is an arbitrary interference with the liberty of contract."

If equality between employer and employee is assumed, the *Lochner* conclusion with regard to legislative interference with such equality follows without too much difficulty. "As between persons sui juris," asks an 1899 state opinion, "what right has the legislature to assume that one class has the need of protection against another?" To the courts at the turn of the century, laws regulating the conditions of employment could be described (as state courts actually did describe them) as putting laborers under "guardianship," as making them "wards of the state," as stamping them as "imbeciles," and as "an insulting attempt to put the laborer under a legislative tutelage . . . degrading to his manhood."

In our own day, such characterizations seem quaintly ludicrous, for we have come to realize that the theory upon which they are based is wholly out of line with actuality. The Supreme Court in a 1908 case could be characterized by Roscoe Pound as dealing with the relation between employer and employee in railway transportation, as if the parties were individual farmers haggling over the sale of a horse. Such an approach—treating a modern industrial problem as if it were only a matter of two neighbors bargaining in the rural, agricultural community of a century ago—was rendered obsolete by the reality of the modern industrial society.

The Supreme Court's use, in the first part of this century, of substantive due process to strike down state statutes interfering with freedom of contract in the conduct of business and labor relations was paralleled by its restrictive approach to the commerce clause. In the landmark case of *Gibbons v. Ogden* (we saw in Chapter III), Chief Justice Marshall had construed the clause in an expansive manner in line with his consistent concern to insure to the nation the powers needed for effective government. To him the commerce which the Congress could regulate included all business dealings which were interstate in character or affected such dealings. And the power to regulate was the plenary power to prescribe the rule by which commerce is to be governed.

After Marshall's time, the Supreme Court tended greatly to limit the broad scope which he had given to the congressional commerce power. This tendency was not, at first, of great practical importance, for the outstanding fact about the federal commerce power during most of the first part of the nation's history was the relative rarity of its exercise. For a century, the Supreme Court itself stated in 1942, there was "little occasion for the affirmative exercise of the commerce power and the influence of the Clause on American life and law was a negative one."

But the same factors which led the states to seek to intervene in the economic sphere toward the end of the last century also induced similar activity on the part of the Federal Government. The abuses of industrialism increasingly called forth regulatory laws from Washington—starting with the Interstate Commerce Act of 1887, the pioneer regulatory statute based upon the commerce power. It was with the enactment of that law, the high bench has said, "that the interstate commerce power began to exert positive influence on American law and life."

It was at this point, when the Federal Government felt called upon to intervene actively in the economic sphere, that the judicial tendency to narrow the extended reach which Marshall had given to the commerce power became of the greatest consequence. Marshall's interpretation of the commerce clause, we saw, gave a broad construction both to the term "commerce" and to the congressional power to "regulate." The post-Marshall Court restricted the meaning of both of these commerce clause terms.

In the first place, the Court withdrew from the conception of commerce a large part of the economic activity of the nation. Of especial significance in this respect were a series of decisions holding that production or manufacturing was not commerce subject to congressional authority, even though such production or manufacturing was undertaken with the intent that the products should be transported across state lines. According to the high bench's new notion, production itself was a purely local act divorced from the flow of interstate commerce and hence subject only to state regulation. And, in the Court's theory, the same came to be true of mining and agriculture. These, too, were purely local events, not part of the interstate commerce subject to federal control, even where the end result was the shipment of the mineral or farm products to other states. In the view of the Court, as it developed in the first part of the present century, it made no difference that the manufacture, or mining, or agriculture—what it considered the purely local activity—had an effect upon interstate commerce, unless the effect was so immediate that the Court considered it to be "direct."

What this restricted conception of the commerce that Congress could reach meant in practice was amply shown by the 1895 case of *United States v. E. C. Knight Co.,* more popularly styled the *Sugar Trust Case.* That case arose out of the first important prosecution brought by the government under the Sherman Anti-Trust Act of 1890. The defendant was a company which had obtained a virtual monopoly over the manufacture of refined sugar in this country. The complaint charged that defendant had violated the Sherman Act by its acquisition of the stock of its principal competitors, several sugar-refining companies in Pennsylvania. The Supreme Court held, however, that such acquisition could not be reached by the federal commerce power. The monopolistic acts alleged related only to manufacturing, which under the view already stated was not within the scope of the commerce clause.

According to Justice Harlan, who dissented, the effect of the *Knight* decision was to defeat the main object for which the Sherman Act was passed. It was not, indeed, until the *Knight* restriction was substantially watered down that the Anti-Trust Law itself could effectively be employed as a weapon against practices in restraint of trade. "The Knight decision," said the Supreme Court a half century after *Knight,* "made the statute a dead letter . . . and had its full force remained unmodified, the Act today would be a weak instrument, as would also the power of Congress, to reach evils in all the vast operations of our gigantic national industrial system antecedent to interstate sale and transportation of manufactured products."

But the Supreme Court, in the period under discussion, went even further in restricting the broad scope which the Marshall Court had given to the congressional commerce power. In addition to narrowing the connotation of "commerce," the Court moved sharply away from the meaning Marshall had given to the verb "regulate" in the constitutional clause. To Marshall and his associates, it will be recalled, the power to regulate was the complete power to control. The sole question for the Court was whether what was at issue was actually a regulation of commerce; if it was, it was valid under the plenary congressional power, regardless of the motives which had called forth the exercise of such power. Here, too, the high tribunal at the turn of the century differed. In its view, the fact that regulation of commerce was involved did not necessarily conclude the case. The Court had to determine also whether the end for which the Congress had exerted its commerce power was itself one toward which congressional authority could lawfully be directed.

The classic case to illustrate this limitation of the term "regulate" in the commerce clause during the period under discussion is the 1918 case of *Hammer v. Dagenhart* (usually known as the *Child Labor Case*), which became one of the *causes célèbres* of our constitutional law. It involved the constitutionality of a federal statute which prohibited the transportation in interstate commerce of goods made in factories that employed children under a specified age. This law clearly purported to be limited to the confines of the express power of the Congress to regulate interstate commerce. But there is no doubt that, though it did not in its terms seek to interfere with local production or manufacturing, the real purpose of Congress in enacting the statute was to suppress child labor in this country. With goods produced by children denied their interstate market, child labor could not continue upon a widespread scale.

To the majority of the Supreme Court, the congressional purpose rendered the law at issue invalid. By its enactment of the statute, the federal legislature was seeking primarily to regulate the manner in which manufacturing was carried on; such manufacturing, we have seen, under the restricted meaning of the Court, was not commerce which could be reached by congressional authority. "In our view," reads the *Child Labor Case* opinion, "the necessary effect of this act is, by means of a prohibition against the movement in interstate commerce of ordinary commercial commodities, to regulate the hours of labor of children in factories and mines within the States, a purely state authority." The Congress could not, in other words, even by an act whose terms were specifically limited to the regulation of interstate commerce, use its commerce power to exert regulatory authority over matters like manufacturing which were not, within the Court's restricted notion, commerce.

The narrow judicial approach had a particularly distressing

result in the *Child Labor Case*. "If there is any matter," asserted Justice Holmes in his dissent there, "upon which civilized countries have agreed . . . it is the evil of premature and excessive child labor." Yet the practical result of the Supreme Court's decision was to render effective regulation of child labor all but impossible. In a country like the United States, if a practice like child labor is to be dealt with effectually, it must be by national regulation. By rigidly excluding the Federal Government from exercising regulatory authority, the *Child Labor Case* virtually decreed that child labor should be left only to whatever controls were afforded by the workings of an unrestrained system of laissez faire. The United States alone, among nations, was precluded from taking effective action against an evil so widely censured by civilized opinion.

This was the background of high-bench jurisprudence when the Administration of Franklin D. Roosevelt took office. Its program sought to resuscitate the depressed economy by the extended intervention of the Federal Government. The New Deal measures involved the very negation of laissez faire. They meant a degree of governmental control from Washington far greater than any previously attempted. If the country was to go forward, said President Roosevelt in his inaugural address in 1932, "we must move as a trained and loyal army willing to sacrifice for the good of a common discipline, because without such discipline no progress is made, no leadership becomes effective."

The effort to move the nation forward, however, came up against the restricted view of the commerce power which had been developed by the Supreme Court. The fate in the high tribunal of much of the New Deal legislation may be seen dramatically in the 1936 case of *Carter v. Carter Coal Co.,* where the Supreme Court had before it a federal law regulating the bituminous coal industry by price fixing, proscription of unfair trade practices, and prescription of labor conditions. In declaring this law, and particularly its labor provisions, invalid, the majority of the Court relied directly upon the narrowed notion of commerce already referred to.

The *Carter* opinion rests upon the proposition that mere manufacturing or mining does not constitute commerce: "The local character of mining, of manufacturing and of crop growing is a fact, and remains a fact, whatever may be done with the products." The effect of the labor provisions of the challenged law, said the Court, primarily falls upon production, not upon commerce. Commerce was said to be a thing apart from the relation of employer and employee, which in all producing occupations was said to be purely local in character. And, in the highest Court's view, it made no difference that labor practices in the gigantic coal industry clearly had an effect upon interstate commerce. To the Court, this effect was not "direct" enough; the direct effect was upon production and, then, the production itself affected commerce.

The highest tribunal had previously rendered decisions nullifying the two most important anti-Depression measures of the New Deal: the National Industrial Recovery Act and the Agricultural Adjustment Act. The NIRA was held beyond the reach of congressional power as applied to small wholesale poultry dealers in Brooklyn. The business done by them was purely local in character, even though the poultry handled by them came from outside the state. And, under the high bench's approach, it did not make any difference that there was some effect upon interstate commerce by the business being regulated. Similarly, in holding the AAA unconstitutional, the Court relied upon the proposition that agriculture, like manufacturing or mining, is not commerce and hence is immune from federal control. In both cases, the restricted post-Marshall meaning of the term "commerce" had been used to deny to the Congress authority over most vital aspects of the national economy.

The restrictive interpretation of the commerce power in these New Deal decisions was catastrophic in its consequences upon effective governmental regulation. Elimination of manufacturing, mining, agriculture, and other productive industries from the reach of the commerce clause rendered the Congress powerless to deal with problems in those fields, however pressing they might become. And so, as Justice Robert H. Jackson stated, in characterizing the effect of the *Carter* decision, "a national government that has power, through the Federal Trade Commission, to prohibit the giving of prizes with penny candy shipped by the manufacturer from one state to another, was powerless to deal with the causes of critical stoppages in the gigantic bituminous coal industry."

This comment drew special pertinence from the grim economic background behind the New Deal measures such as that at issue in *Carter*. Giant industries prostrate, crises in production and consumption throughout the country, the economy in a state of virtual collapse—if ever there was a need for exertion of federal power, it was after the collapse of 1929. If federal power was not to be as broad as that need, it meant that the nation was helpless in the face of economic disaster.

Under the *Carter* opinion, all this was irrelevant. If there was no "direct" effect upon commerce, in the narrow sense in which the Supreme Court used the term "commerce," there was no federal power to regulate—regardless of the size of the industry or the magnitude of the problems involved. "The distinction between a direct and an indirect effect," asserted the *Carter* Court, "turns, not upon the magnitude of either the cause or the effect, but entirely upon the manner in which the effect has been brought about. If the production by one man of a single ton of coal intended for interstate sale and shipment, and actually so sold and shipped, affects interstate commerce indirectly, the effect does not become direct by multiplying the tonnage, or increasing the number of men employed, or adding to the expense or complexities of the business, or by all combined."

This aspect of *Carter* was the veritable *reductio ad absurdum* of the high Court's restricted commerce-clause approach. Under it, the matter of degree had no bearing upon the question of federal power: there was no difference between the mining of one ton of coal and ten million tons of coal, so far as the effect on commerce was concerned. Production was purely local. Even though there was a production crisis throughout the country, it could not be dealt with on a national level.

It is true that the decisions in cases like *Carter* did not affect the authority of the states to control production within their own boundaries. But state power must necessarily end at the state limits and is hardly competent to cope with modern economic activity which so often extends over more than one state. In addition, regulation limited to that exerted by the states must, of necessity, vary from state to state. State control cannot in most cases have the uniform character necessary for efficacious economic regulation.

If a national industry like bituminous coal production is effectively to be regulated, it must be by regulation that is national in character. As a federal judge has expressed it, "To say that the production of products distributed on a national scale can be effectively controlled by the states is both constitutionally and economically absurd. To deny power in such a field to the national government is tantamount to saying there shall be no legislation concerning them." Under the cases we have discussed, nevertheless, national regulation was precluded. In effect, then, the result of the restricted conception of the commerce clause taken by the Supreme Court was to prevent effectual economic regulation in this country.

Almost needless to say, the recession from the Marshall conception fitted in perfectly with the laissez-faire theory of governmental function that dominated political and economic thinking for a century after the death of the great Chief Justice. To bar federal intervention, as the Supreme Court did in these cases, was all but to exclude the possibility of any effective regulation in them. This was, of course, exactly what was demanded by the advocates of laissez faire; for, to them, the economic system could function properly only if it was permitted to operate free from governmental interference.

The Constitution, states Justice Holmes in a celebrated passage, "is not intended to embody a particular economic theory, whether of paternalism and the organic relation of the citizen to the state or of laissez faire." At the same time, it was most difficult for judges not to assume that the basic document was intended to embody the dominant economic beliefs of their own day. The Constitution, to cite another famous Holmes statement, may not enact Mr. Herbert Spencer's *Social Statics*. But the Supreme Court's narrow notion of commerce was a necessary complement to the translation of Spencerian economics into American constitutional law.

The decisions culminating in *Carter* presented a disturbing paradox. As industry became more and more interstate in character, the power of the Congress to regulate was given a narrower and narrower interpretation. The coal industry after 1929, whose regulation was at issue in *Carter,* was one for which national intervention had become a categorical imperative of survival. The market and the states had found the problems of the industry beyond their competence. The choice was between federal action and chaos. A system of constitutional law that required the latter could hardly endure. As the high Court expressed it in 1948, *Carter* and similar decisions, "embracing the same artificially drawn lines, produced a series of consequences for the exercise of national power over industry conducted on a national scale which the evolving nature of our industrialism foredoomed to reversal."

IX

CONSTITUTIONAL REVOLUTION

IN POLITICAL, as in natural, science, extremes beget extremes. Action which moves too far in one direction ultimately provokes an equivalent reaction in the opposite direction. Even an institution as august as the United States Supreme Court cannot escape the law of the pendulum. If, in the generation before 1937, the high bench construed the doctrine of judicial supremacy so as to give itself the virtual powers of a super-legislature, in the period since that time, the Court's authority vis-à-vis the substantive power of the Congress has drastically diminished.

Early in 1937, a remarkable reversal in the Supreme Court's attitude toward the New Deal program took place. Before that time (1934–1936), the Court rendered twelve decisions declaring invalid legislative measures of the New Deal; starting in April, 1937, that tribunal upheld every New Deal law presented to it, including some that were basically similar to earlier statutes which it had nullified. It is, in truth, not too farfetched to assert that, in 1937, there took place a veritable revolution in the jurisprudence of the Supreme Court—a revolution which Corwin has appropriately characterized as "Constitutional Revolution, Ltd."

It is all too facile to state that the 1937 change in the high bench's jurisprudence was only a direct protective response to President Roosevelt's Court Reorganization Plan—to assert, as did so many contemporary wags, that "a switch in time saved Nine." It would be idle to deny that the furor over the President's proposal did have repercussions within the marble halls of the Supreme Court building. The members of the Court are not demigods far above the sweaty crowd; they are, to refer to Bryce's celebrated truism, "only men." As such, it is scarcely surprising that they were intimately concerned with a proposal that affected so directly the institution of which they were a part.

This was especially true of Chief Justice Charles Evans Hughes, who did not hesitate to play an active role in the struggle to defeat the President's "court-packing" plan. There is little doubt that the Chief Justice helped persuade a majority of the Court to liberalize its case law, in order to help preserve that tribunal in all its institutional strength. As President Roosevelt himself expressed it, "It would be a little naive to refuse to recognize some connection between these 1937 decisions and the Supreme Court fight." Indeed, the new decisions of the Court, in F.D.R.'s own words, "did more than anything else to bring about the defeat of the [Court Reorganization] plan in the halls of Congress." It was surely not unnatural of the Justices to reconstrue the law so as to help bring about such a result.

At the same time, it would be wholly to misconceive the nature of the Supreme Court and its manner of operation as a judicial tribunal to assume that the 1937 change in jurisprudence was solely the result of the President's "court-packing" plan. In actuality, the pre-1937 decisions of the Court which so greatly restricted the powers of the national government were based upon an outmoded conception of the proper role of government. Even at the time of the *Lochner* case in 1905, to repeat the statement of Justice Holmes, dissenting, there, the case was "decided upon an economic theory which a large part of the country does not entertain." By the time of the New Deal, that theory, though still persisted in by a bare majority of the Supreme Court, had been expressly repudiated by the people and by the President and the Congress whom they had voted into office.

The high Court's conception of the proper constitutional role of government may well have been sound when it was first formulated in the 1890's. It was utterly inconsistent with an era which demanded ever-expanding governmental power. It could, as a practical matter, be maintained only when the exercise of public authority was dominated by the concept of laissez faire.

"Leviathan hath two swords: war and justice," stated Hobbes in a famous passage. The need to deal effectively with the great economic crisis of the early 1930's had, however, made it plain that the government armory had to include much more than these two elementary weapons. Before the New Deal, government was chiefly negative: its main task (apart from defense) was to keep the ring and maintain some semblance of fair play while private interests asserted themselves freely. Under the Roosevelt Administration, government became positive in a new sense. Before then, the body politic acted as policeman, soldier, and judge. Since 1933, government has had to act also as doctor, nurse, insurance supplier, house builder, chemist, power supplier, town planner, pensions distributor, economic controller, benefactor of labor and agriculture, and in a whole host of other capacities.

For the government to execute effectively the manifold functions which economic and social exigencies required it to assume, it had to intervene in social and economic affairs upon a national scale. Governmental action limited to the local level could hardly prove efficacious where problems national in scope had to be dealt with.

For the Supreme Court Canute-like to attempt to hold back indefinitely the waves of ever-increasing governmental authority was for it to set itself an impossible task. "Looking back," declared Justice Owen J. Roberts (the man whose switch is, more than anything else, said to have "saved the Nine" in 1937) in 1951, "it is difficult to see how the Court could have resisted the popular urge for uniform standards throughout the country—for what in effect was a unified economy." The laissez-faire doctrine, upon which the operation of American government had been essentially based since the founding of the Republic, had proved wholly inadequate to meet pressing economic problems. The national economy could be resuscitated only by extended federal intervention.

For the government in Washington to be able to exercise regulatory authority upon the necessary national scale, it was essential that the Supreme Court liberalize its construction of the Constitution. To quote Justice Roberts again, "An insistence by the Court on holding federal power to what seemed its appropriate orbit when the Constitution was adopted might have resulted in even more radical changes in our dual structure than those which have been gradually accomplished through the extension of the limited jurisdiction conferred on the federal government."

That the Supreme Court would ultimately recognize the inevitable was itself inevitable. Benjamin Nathan Cardozo has shown how the results reached in cases like the decisions discussed in the last chapter were due to the judicial choice of starting points:

> A problem in the choice of methods lay back of the problem of law, and determined its solution. On the one hand, the right of property, as it was known to the fathers of the republic, was posited as permanent and absolute. Impairment was not to be suffered except within narrow limits of history and precedent. No experiment was to be made along new lines of social betterment. The image was a perfect sphere. The least dent or abrasion was a subtraction from its essence. Given such premises, the conclusion is inevitable. The statute becomes an illegitimate assault upon rights assured to the individual against the encroachments of society. The method of logic . . . is at work in all its plenitude.

By 1937, it had become clear that formal logic alone, based upon outmoded starting points, had become inadequate as the instrument of advance. Even judges whose *logos* had been based upon Spencerian dogmas (or at least a majority of such judges) had come to see that the philosophy upon which they had based their decisions had been left behind by the changed needs of a new era. "The meaning of the Constitution does not change with the ebb and flow of economic events," plaintively declared a member of the old Court majority in 1937, just after the Court had begun its historic shift. But, though the words of the basic document have remained essentially what they were in 1787, the high bench itself has come to recognize that the proper interpretation of that instrument does change to meet the new demands imposed by changed external conditions. The Constitution must be capable of adaptation to needs that were wholly unforeseen by the Founding Fathers; else, it is less a document intended to endure through the ages than a government's suicide pact.

The 1937 reversal in the jurisprudence of the Supreme Court reflected changes in legal ideology common to the entire American legal profession. The extreme individualistic philosophy upon which the Justices had been nurtured has been shaken to its foundations during the present century. If Spencerian laissez faire gave way on the bench to the judicial pragmatism of Justice Holmes, it was only because a similar movement had taken place in the country as a whole. That there was a lag between the change in the country and the change in the Court cannot, of course, be denied. Such a lag is well-nigh inherent in the functioning of any judicial tribunal which is compelled by changing external conditions to make fundamental modifications in its case law. It may indeed be said that this is a necessary aspect of the American system of judicial review. That it may, at times, constitute a great danger of the system cannot be denied: the basic conservatism of the Court may make it difficult for its members to make the necessary accommodation before it is too late.

In 1937 the danger referred to was averted by the high bench's reversal in jurisprudence. And even then, it should be noted, a hard core of the old majority utterly refused to alter its views—which shows how narrow the actual margin of change was in the Court. In reality, it was the recognition by two Justices (primarily Roberts and, to a lesser extent, Hughes) of the need for increased national governmental power that made for the swing-over in the high tribunal. "Years ago," wrote an eminent constitutional-law professor about the Court of the mid-1930's, "that learned lawyer John Selden in talking of 'Council' observed: 'They talk (but blasphemously enough) that the Holy Ghost is President of their General Councils when the truth is, the odd Man is still the Holy Ghost.' " It was the conversion of "odd men" Roberts and Hughes that made the constitutional revolution of 1937 possible.

Yet, narrow though the margin for change may have been, there is little doubt that there was a real conversion in the new majority of the Supreme Court and that its effects do justify the characterization of "constitutional revolution." It is usually overlooked that the decisions first signaling the reversal in high-bench jurisprudence were, in all probability, reached before the President had even announced his Court Reorganization Plan. On March 29, 1937, the Chief Justice announced a decision upholding a state minimum-wage law, basically similar to one which the Court had held to be beyond the power of both states and nation to enact only nine months previously. According to one who then sat at the government counsel table, "the spectacle of the Court that day frankly and completely reversing itself and striking down its opinion but a few months' old was a moment never to be forgotten." But, though the Court's confession of error was announced a month after the President's proposal, the case itself appears to have been decided in conference among the Justices about a month before the "court-packing" plan was announced.

The circumstantial evidence available to us on this point strongly bears out the statement made some years later by Chief Justice Hughes to his authorized biographer: "The President's proposal had not the slightest effect on our decision." The decision marking the first drastic change in the pre-1937 case law had not been influenced by the Roosevelt plan because it had actually been made within the high bench before the publication of the President's proposal. All of which tends to bear out the view that the Court's jurisprudence was ripe for reversal and that such reversal might well have occurred even without the pressure of the "court-packing" plan.

March 29, 1937, as already indicated, saw the upholding of a state minimum-wage law. Though not directly concerned with national power, the Court did expressly overrule a 1923 precedent denying congressional authority to fix wages; hence, the decision was a substantial step forward from the point of view of advocates of increased national power. On the same day, the Court dealt squarely with federal statutes similar to several annulled in the 1934–1936 period. This time the Court upheld laws providing for farm debtors' relief, collective bargaining in the nation's railroads, and a penalizing tax on firearms analogous to that it had stricken down under the Agricultural Adjustment Act. Well could a leading New Dealer chortle, "What a day! To labor, minimum-wage laws and collective bargaining; to farmers, relief in bankruptcy;

to law enforcement, the firearms control. The Court was on the march!"

These cases, in Volume 300 of the *Supreme Court Reports,* were to prove but the prelude to an even more drastic revolution in constitutional jurisprudence. To demonstrate the extent of the judicial revolution, one has, to use the method stated by Corwin, only to "turn to Volume 301 of the *United States Supreme Court Reports,* a volume which has a single counterpart in the Court's annals. I mean Volume 11 of *Peters's Reports,* wherein is recorded the somewhat lesser revolution in our constitutional law precisely 100 years earlier, which followed upon Taney's succession to Marshall."

On page 1 of Volume 301 U.S. is printed the decision of the highest tribunal in the great case of *National Labor Relations Board v. Jones & Laughlin Steel Corp*. In this case, the constitutionality of the National Labor Relations Act of 1935 was upheld. Robert H. Jackson termed the decision there the most far-reaching victory ever won on behalf of labor in the Supreme Court. This was no overstatement, for the 1935 act was the Magna Charta of the American labor movement. It guaranteed the right of employees to organize collectively in unions and made it an unfair labor practice prohibited by law for employers to interfere with such right or to refuse to bargain collectively with the representatives chosen by their employees.

The Labor Relations Act was intended to apply to industries throughout the nation, to those engaged in production and manufacture as well as to those engaged in commerce, literally speaking. But this appeared to bring it directly in conflict with the Supreme Court decisions drastically limiting the scope of the Federal Government's authority over interstate commerce, including some of the 1934–1936 period on which the ink was scarcely dry. This was particularly true of the Court's decision nullifying the National Industrial Recovery Act, which had denied power in the Congress to regulate local business activities, even though they affected interstate commerce.

In the *Jones & Laughlin* case, these precedents were not followed: "These cases," laconically stated the Court, "are not controlling here." Instead, the high tribunal gave the federal power over interstate commerce its maximum sweep. Mines, mills, and factories, whose activities had formerly been decided as being "local," and hence immune from federal regulation, were now held to affect interstate commerce directly enough to justify congressional control. There is little doubt that, as the dissenting Justices in *Jones & Laughlin* protested, the Congress in the Labor Relations Act exercised a power of control over purely local industry beyond anything theretofore deemed permissible. In truth, as the dissenters accurately stated, in characterizing the effect of the Court's reinterpretation of the commerce power, "Almost anything—marriage, birth, death—may in some fashion affect commerce."

The *Jones & Laughlin* case was followed some six weeks later by three equally significant decisions, also printed in Volume 301 of the *Supreme Court Reports,* upholding the constitutionality of one of the most important of the New Deal innovations, the Social Security Act of 1935. That law, which for the first time brought the Federal Government extensively into the field of social insurance, had been held unconstitutional by the lower court. The Supreme Court, however, in a precedent-making opinion by Justice Cardozo, reversed that tribunal, holding that the scheme of old-age benefits provided for by the federal law did not contravene any constitutional prohibition.

In so ruling, the high bench gave the broadest possible scope to the congressional power to tax and spend for the general welfare, even though its reasoning on this point was inconsistent with its earlier decision invalidating the Agricultural Adjustment Act. In addition, the Court upheld the unemployment compensation schemes established under the Social Security Act. The decisions sustaining that law put an end to fears that unemployment insurance and old-age benefit laws might prove to be beyond the power of either states or nation, as minimum-wage regulation had been held to be under the pre-1937 Court. Henceforth the United States was not to be the one great nation powerless to adopt such measures.

The decisions discussed in 301 U.S. constituted the heart of the constitutional revolution of 1937. Breaking with its previous jurisprudence, the Supreme Court upheld the authority of the Federal Government to regulate the entire economy under its commerce power and to use its power to tax and spend to set up comprehensive schemes of social insurance. And, it should be noted, in the light of later criticism of the Court (whose members were subsequently appointed by President Roosevelt) because of its claimed cavalier discard of established precedents, the cases in 301 U.S. were decided before a single Roosevelt-appointed Justice took his seat upon the bench. The most important of the old precedents which so restricted the scope of governmental authority were repudiated by the identical Court which had previously invoked them. There was no change in the Court's personnel until after it provided new precedents that served as a basis for much that the new judges were later to decide.

Critics of the Supreme Court have urged that its recent jurisprudence has vested unprecedented power in the Federal Government, thus completely upsetting the equilibrium between states and nation that earlier Supreme Courts were so careful to maintain. It cannot be denied that this criticism is valid if one looks only at the precedents of the half century or so prior to 1937; some of the decisions after that time, to paraphrase one attorney, discarded "the precedents of fifty years without even the decency of funeral obsequies." Yet, as we saw in the last chapter, the precedents of the pre-1937 period had themselves been based upon a repudiation of earlier precedents. The Court itself had ignored the broad holdings of the Marshall Court in adopting its restrictive interpretation of the congressional commerce power.

According to a contemporary analysis by Robert H. Jackson, the post-1937 decisions of the Supreme Court marked a "retreat to the Constitution" by the highest tribunal. This view may express too sanguine an opinion of the Court's new decisions; but, resting as these decisions did upon a broad construction of the commerce clause, they certainly did, at the least, mark a return by the Court to the Marshall conception of the congressional commerce power.

This can be observed from the *Jones & Laughlin* decision, already seen to be the landmark case of the constitutional revolution of 1937. In *Jones & Laughlin,* we saw, the high bench upheld the constitutionality of the National Labor Relations Act, under which the Congress had enacted a comprehensive scheme for the regulation of labor relations in the American economy. The difficulty in the case arose from the fact that the company being regulated was engaged only in the business of manufacturing iron and steel. Under the narrow interpretation which had been given to the commerce clause only the year before in the *Carter Coal Co.* case (Chapter VIII), such manufacturing was not commerce and hence not subject to congressional control. Nor, under the *Carter* approach, we have seen, did it make any difference that the company being regulated was an industrial giant whose operations clearly had an effect upon interstate commerce. Such effect could not, in the *Carter* view, give Congress authority over purely local production. It is not surprising that the lower court held that the Labor Relations Act lay beyond the range of federal power. In fact, considering the Supreme Court's resolute language in *Carter,* it is somewhat surprising that the high tribunal should have even permitted argument on the point. Yet, not only was extensive argument allowed, but the Court itself, in its decision, completely abandoned its previous restrictive approach to the meaning of commerce and returned to the broad sweep which John Marshall had given to the term more than a century earlier.

The company regulated in the *Jones & Laughlin* case relied directly upon the decisions holding that manufacturing in itself was not commerce, arguing that because of them the industrial relations and activities in its manufacturing department were not subject to federal regulation. Chief Justice Hughes, in a masterful opinion for the majority of the Court, stated, however, that the fact that the employees here concerned were engaged in production was not determinative: "The close and intimate effect which brings the subject within the reach of federal power may be due to activities in relation to productive industry although the industry when separately viewed is local."

In the *Jones & Laughlin* case, there is no doubt—any more than there was in a case like *Carter v. Carter Coal Co.*—that the production regulated affected interstate commerce. But here the

Court declared that, in view of the company's far-flung activities, it would be idle to say that such effect was only indirect: "When industries organize themselves on a national scale, making their relation to interstate commerce the dominant factor in their activities, how can it be maintained that their industrial labor relations constitute a forbidden field into which Congress may not enter when it is necessary to protect interstate commerce from the paralyzing consequences of industrial war?"

The Court's rationale here, as already emphasized, rests upon a repudiation of the limited connotation of commerce upon which decisions like that in the *Carter Coal Co.* case had been based. The *Carter* opinion had declared that production was not commerce; the *Jones & Laughlin* opinion held production to be subject to congressional regulation under the commerce power. *Carter* had found immaterial the evils which had induced the Congress to act and the effect of these evils upon interstate commerce, declaring that, extensive though such effect might be, it was only secondary and indirect; *Jones & Laughlin* was fully cognizant of the catastrophic effect which industrial strife could have upon interstate commerce, and asserted categorically that such effect could not be dismissed as only indirect.

The *Jones & Laughlin* decision marks a definite break with the pre-1937 Court's imposition of restrictions upon the scope of the term "commerce"; under it, as just pointed out, manufacturing as such is not automatically excluded from the reach of the commerce power. Later cases extend the *Jones & Laughlin* approach to mining and agriculture.

In 1940, the Supreme Court upheld a new congressional act regulating the bituminous coal industry, similar in many ways to that which had been annulled in the *Carter Coal Co.* case. This time there was no doubt that coal mining was not considered immune from the commerce power. "The regulatory provisions," reads the Court's opinion, "are clearly within the power of Congress under the commerce clause of the Constitution. . . . Congress under the commerce clause is not impotent to deal with what it may consider to be dire consequences of laissez-faire." Similarly, in 1939, the Court held valid the Agricultural Adjustment Act of

1938, whose basic features were not unlike those of the law of the same name condemned in 1936.

Having removed the post-Marshall restrictions upon the meaning of commerce, the highest Court then proceeded, in the period after 1937, to return to the great Chief Justice's view of the congressional power to *regulate* under the commerce clause as a complete one. That power, said Chief Justice Hughes in his *Jones & Laughlin* opinion, is plenary and may be exerted to foster, protect, control, and restrain commerce. That being the case, it seems clear that there has been no room in the post-1937 Court for a decision like that in the *Child Labor Case* (Chapter VIII), which invalidated an admitted regulation of interstate commerce because the congressional purpose had been to regulate indirectly local economic activities which were beyond the reach of the federal commerce power.

After decisions in 1938 and 1939 eroding the constitutional basis of the *Child Labor Case,* the Supreme Court in 1941 expressly overruled that case. This occurred in *United States v. Darby,* where the legality of the Fair Labor Standards Act of 1938 was at issue. That law provided for the fixing of minimum wages and maximum hours by a federal agency. It prohibited the shipment in interstate commerce of goods manufactured by employees whose wages are less than the prescribed minimum or whose hours of work are more than the prescribed maximum. As such, it was not unlike the law at issue in the *Child Labor Case,* which had prohibited the transportation in interstate commerce of goods produced by child labor. In its *Darby* decision, none the less, the Court refused to follow the reasoning of the *Child Labor Case:* "The reasoning and conclusion of the Court's opinion there cannot be reconciled with the conclusion which we have reached, that the power of Congress under the Commerce Clause is plenary to exclude any article from interstate commerce subject only to the specific prohibitions of the Constitution."

The *Darby* Court was, of course, aware that the motive and purpose of the congressional prohibition at issue were to make effective the legislative policy of eliminating substandard labor conditions by closing the markets of interstate commerce to goods produced under such conditions. In this sense, the effect of the challenged law was clearly a regulation of the wages and hours of those engaged in what had formerly been held to be only local production and manufacturing.

But the whole point about the *Darby* decision is that, under it, the end toward which a congressional exercise of regulatory power over commerce is directed is irrelevant. According to Justice Stone's opinion for a now unanimous Court, "The motive and purpose of a regulation of interstate commerce are matters for the legislative judgment upon the exercise of which the Constitution places no restriction and over which the courts are given no control." Thus the high bench definitely disowned the *Child Labor Case* thesis that the motive of the prohibition could operate to deprive the congressional regulation of its constitutional validity. Instead the Court relied directly upon the Marshall definition of the power to regulate commerce as the power "to prescribe the rule by which commerce is governed." "Whatever their motive and purpose," declared the *Darby* opinion, "regulations of commerce which do not infringe some constitutional prohibition are within the plenary power conferred on Congress by the Commerce Clause." Thus had the wheel of constitutional construction swung full circle in the century after the death of John Marshall.

The decisions rendered by the highest tribunal in 1937 can be characterized as embodying a constitutional revolution not only because they recognized in the Federal Government significant substantive powers that had theretofore been denied. Even more important perhaps to one concerned with the workings of the Supreme Court is the fact that they inaugurated a drastic shift in the balance that had previously existed between the Court and the other branches of the government. The pre-1937 interpretation of the doctrine of judicial supremacy had been dominated by the primacy of the Supreme Court, culminating, as we saw in the last chapter, in the Court's review of the desirability of the early New Deal legislation. Since 1937, the Court has receded to a more subdued position.

Where the high bench prior to 1937 set itself up as Supreme Censor of the wisdom of challenged legislation, it has since that time more or less adopted the view formerly expressed in dissent by Justice Holmes as to what its function should be vis-à-vis the legislature. The Holmesian view was neatly expressed in his comment to Chief Justice Stone: "About seventy-five years ago I learnt that I was not God. And so, when the people . . . want to do something I can't find anything in the Constitution expressly forbidding them to do, I say, whether I like it or not, 'Godammit, let 'em do it!' "

In this comment is expressed the essence of the self-restraint which now prevails in the Supreme Court. Unless the statute at issue patently violates an express constitutional provision, it will be upheld. Under the present approach, there is no place for the super-legislature conception of the Court's role that prevailed prior to 1937. Instead, the high tribunal is controlled by the conviction that it is an awesome thing to strike down an act of the elected representatives of the people, and that its power to do so should not be exercised save where the occasion is clear beyond fair debate. As Justice Holmes expressed it in a celebrated dissent, a statute should not be ruled invalid "unless it can be said that a rational and fair man necessarily would admit that the statute proposed would infringe fundamental principles as they have been understood by the traditions of our people and our law."

In the Holmesian view, the test to be applied is whether a reasonable legislator—the congressional version of the "reasonable man"—could have adopted a law like that at issue. Is the statute as applied so clearly arbitrary or capricious that legislators acting reasonably could not have believed it to be necessary or appropriate for the public welfare?

Under the earlier approach, the test was whether the high Court itself thought the statute was desirable. Now the Justices look only to see whether there was a rational basis for the challenged legislative action. In the pre-1937 attitude, the desirability of a statute was determined as an objective fact by the Court on its own independent judgment. Today a more subjective test is applied, i.e., could rational legislators have regarded the statute as a reasonable method of reaching the desired result? "It can never be emphasized too much," Justice Frankfurter has declared, "that one's own opinion about the wisdom or evil of a law should be excluded altogether when one is doing one's duty on the bench. The only opinion of our own even looking in that direction that is material is our opinion whether legislators could in reason have enacted such a law."

The change just outlined in the Supreme Court's approach to the manner of exercise of its review power has had tremendous impact upon the doctrine of substantive due process—the basic foundation upon which the pre-1937 judicial supremacy had been built. Few today doubt that the high tribunal went too far before 1937 in its application of the doctrine of substantive due process, or that the Court since that time has been correct in deliberately discarding its predecessors' extreme due-process philosophy. There is, to paraphrase a 1945 opinion of Justice Hugo L. Black, a strong emotional appeal in words like "fair and reasonable" or "freedom of contract." But these words were not chosen by those who wrote either the Constitution or the Fourteenth Amendment as a measuring rod for the Supreme Court to use in invalidating state laws. It is not for a judicial tribunal to set itself up as judge of the wisdom or desirability of measures taken by government to deal with supposed economic evils.

The due process clause was not intended to prevent legislatures from choosing whether to regulate or leave their economies to the blind operation of uncontrolled economic forces, futile or even noxious though the particular choice might seem to the individual judge. Economic views of confined validity are not to be treated as though the Framers had enshrined them in the Constitution. "The Fourteenth Amendment," as Justice Stone protested in 1936, "has no more embedded in the Constitution our preference for some particular set of economic beliefs than it has adopted, in the name of liberty, the system of theology which we may happen to approve."

In his dissent in the *Lochner* case, as noted earlier, Justice Holmes asserted, "This case is decided upon an economic theory which a large part of the country does not entertain." In the period since 1937, both the economic and legal theories upon which *Lochner* rested have been repudiated by the Supreme Court. Early in 1937, the high tribunal overruled its earlier holdings that a minimum-wage law violated due process by impairing freedom of contract between employers and employees. "What is this freedom?" asked the Court's opinion. "The Constitution does not speak of freedom of contract. It speaks of liberty and prohibits the deprivation of liberty without due process of law. In prohibiting that deprivation the Constitution does not recognize an absolute and uncontrollable liberty." The liberty safeguarded by the Constitution is liberty in a society which requires the protection of the law against evils which menace the health, safety, morals, or welfare of the people. Regulation adopted in the interests of the community, the Court concluded, is due process.

The extent to which the post-1937 high Court has followed the view that regulation adopted in the interest of the community is consistent with due process is shown by an important 1952 decision. At issue there was a Missouri statute which provided that any employee entitled to vote might absent himself from his employment for four hours on election days and that it was unlawful for his employer to deduct wages for that absence. It was argued that such a law constituted an invalid deprivation of the employer's property without due process. Such an argument, said the Court, is reminiscent of the philosophy of *Lochner v. New York* and other like due-process decisions of the pre-1937 period.

To be sure, the Missouri law requires the employer to pay wages for a period in which the employee performs no services. But that does not mean that it constitutes a taking of property without due process. The statute at issue was seen to be basically similar to a minimum-wage law, like that upheld in 1937. Though not, like the earlier legislation, designed to protect the health and morals of the citizen, this statute is equally enacted in the interest of the community. It is designed to eliminate any penalty for exercising the right of suffrage and to remove a practical obstacle to getting out the vote: "The public welfare is a broad and inclusive concept. The moral, social, economic, and physical well-being of the community is one part of it; the political well-being, another. The police power which is adequate to fix the financial burden for one is adequate for the other."

It is true, the Court conceded, that the judgment of the legislature—that time out for voting should cost the employee nothing

—may be a debatable one. But that is the whole point about the high bench's changed approach to review under the due process clause. Under this clause, the Court leaves debatable issues, as respects business, economic, and social affairs, to legislative decision. "Our recent decisions," declares Justice William O. Douglas, "make plain that we do not sit as a super-legislature to weigh the wisdom of legislation nor to decide whether the policy which it expresses offends the public welfare." A law like that at issue, asserted the opinion, could be invalidated only if the Court were to return to the philosophy held in cases like *Lochner v. New York*.

The decision upholding the Missouri law shows how far the highest tribunal has retreated from that earlier philosophy. It is one thing to uphold a minimum-wage law; yet, because a state may require payment of a minimum wage for hours that are worked, it does not follow that it may compel payment for time that is not worked. All the same, such a law must be upheld under the theory that regulation adopted in the interests of the community is due process. In the Supreme Court's post-1937 view, the state legislatures have constitutional authority to experiment with new techniques; they are entitled to maintain their own standard of the public welfare; they may, within extremely broad limits, control practices in the business-labor field.

Since 1937, the high bench has had but two occasions to overrule directly other substantive due-process decisions of its predecessors. The first occurred in 1941, when a 1928 case voiding a statute regulating the fees charged by employment agencies was overturned; the second in 1963, when a 1917 decision that a business might not be prohibited where regulation of it was feasible was disowned. "We are not," declares the 1963 opinion, "able or willing to draw lines by calling a law 'prohibitory' or 'regulatory.' "

Though, as just stated, the high Court has had no occasion directly to repudiate other specific substantive due-process decisions of the pre-1937 period, there is no doubt that it would do so if the need arose. For decisions like that upholding the Missouri election-pay law show how clearly the Court has rejected the earlier due-process philosophy. From 1890 to 1937, the high bench used the due process clause as a device to enable it to review the desirability of regulatory legislation. In 1955 that tribunal could declare: "The day is gone when this Court uses the Due Process Clause of the Fourteenth Amendment to strike down state laws, regulatory of business and industrial conditions, because they may be unwise, improvident, or out of harmony with a particular school of thought."

Before 1937 the Supreme Court tested state laws by its own judgment of whether they were reasonable, in the light of the overriding bias of the law against unnecessary governmental interferences with the free working of the economic system. Since that time, the Court has tended more and more to defer to the judgment of the legislature on the desirability of the particular law. As already seen, the present tendency is to adopt the test of whether a rational legislator could have regarded the statute as a reasonable method of protecting the public welfare. It is enough, said the Court in its 1955 opinion just quoted, that there is an evil at hand for correction, and that it might be thought that the particular legislative measure was a rational way to correct it.

Interestingly enough, one of the strongest attempts to induce the high Court to return to the pre-1937 notion of due process was made in 1949 by a labor union, which had, of course, been the very economic group most severely affected by the earlier decisions invalidating laws on due process grounds. By 1949, however, the shoe was on the other foot, for at issue then was a so-called "right-to-work" law which forbade employers to enter into closed-shop agreements, obligating themselves to exclude from employment persons not members of unions. This type of law, unlike those that had been at issue in the pre-1937 period, was intended to protect the nonunion worker. It was thus wholly natural for organized labor to challenge its constitutionality; what was more surprising was that it used the sword against social legislation of which it had so often been the victim in earlier days.

The union claimed that the state law at issue deprived both employers and union members of their freedom of contract. This, the Court itself noted, was to ask for a return to the due process philosophy that has been deliberately discarded since 1937. Such a return was one which could not be taken by a Court which adhered to the doctrine that the due process clause is no longer to be so broadly construed that state legislatures are put in a strait jacket when they attempt to suppress business and industrial conditions which they regard as offensive to the public welfare: "Just as we have held that the due process clause erects no obstacle to block legislative protection of union members, we now hold that legislative protection can be afforded non-union workers."

The Supreme Court's due-process decisions since 1937 have, of course, made for a drastic change in the law of judicial review of the constitutionality of legislation. Such departure from the jurisprudence of its predecessors by a judicial tribunal should, to be sure, be suspect as undermining the stability of the law. In the field under discussion, nevertheless, the rejected precedents had themselves been based upon an unwarranted departure from the more limited meaning originally given the due process clause. There is little doubt that, to paraphrase Justice Robert H. Jackson, the 1890–1936 Court had, by its undue expansion of the concept of due process, torn that concept loose from its ancient connotations and, by so doing, had magnified the doctrine of judicial supremacy beyond legitimate bounds. In rejecting the pre-1937 due process philosophy, the high bench has, as Justice Black put it in 1949, "consciously returned closer and closer to the earlier constitutional principle that states have power to legislate against what are found to be injurious practices in their internal commercial and business affairs, so long as their laws do not run afoul of some specific federal constitutional prohibition, or of some valid federal law." In so doing, the Supreme Court has returned to a more reasonable view of the proper scope of judicial power.

X

WAR AND PEACE

"WE MAY WELL WONDER in view of the precedents now established," declared Charles Evans Hughes not long after the end of the First World War, "whether constitutional government as heretofore maintained in this Republic could survive another great war even victoriously waged." Hughes's assertion was, of course, based upon the nation's experience with the second great conflict in its history since the Revolution. World War I had seen the assumption by the nation of authority that was unprecedented in a country that had not theretofore engaged (save perhaps peripherally in its earliest years) in a struggle thus international in scope.

Constitutional developments after the American entry into the First Great War emphasized the executive primacy that, as the Civil War experience had so amply demonstrated, is an inevitable concomitant of national participation in a full-scale war. "This is a war of resources no less than of men, perhaps even more than of men," said President Wilson, and in accord with this viewpoint the most drastic controls over the nation's resources were given him by Congress. Whereas Lincoln in many instances had to act at once without waiting for Congressional authorization to avoid the risk of national disaster, Wilson was largely able to prosecute the war efficiently under the power delegated to him. Indeed, some in Congress wanted to go further and make him "a supreme dictator" over every phase of war activity.

Among the more significant delegations to the President were grants of the power: (1) to order any industry or firm having the facilities to comply to furnish supplies or equipment for the Army in preference to any other commitments at prices named by him, and, in case of default, to seize and operate the plants; (2) to take possession and assume control of any system or systems of transportation; (3) to take over and operate enemy vessels; (4) to raise and organize the armed forces; (5) to designate prohibited places under the Espionage Act; (6) to regulate exports; (7) to control priorities in transportation; (8) to license the importation, manufacture, storage, mining, or distribution of any necessaries; (9) to requisition necessaries for public use; (10) to requisition and take over, for use or operation by the government, any factory, packing house, oil pipeline, mine or other plant, or any part thereof, in or through which any necessaries are or may be manufactured, produced, prepared, or mined, and to operate the same; (11) to regulate the prices of wheat and fuel; (12) to regulate trading and communications with the enemy; (13) to censor communications to foreign countries; (14) to license the use of enemy patents and trade-marks; and (15) to assume control of any telegraph, telephone, marine cable, or radio system.

It was not only during the conflict itself that national primacy was vested in Wilson. Presidential leadership was not limited to the waging of war; it extended as well to the making of peace. The Versailles Treaty fiasco should not make us overlook that the postwar international structure was largely of presidential creation. Wilson's own actions during the war and the making of peace gave practical emphasis to his own characterization of the President, well before he himself served in the highest office, as "one of the great powers of the world."

Yet, vast though the powers of war and peace exercised by Wilson doubtless were, it remained for the Second World War to demonstrate the true extent of presidential primacy under twentieth-century conditions. John Marshall had, with customary acuity, foreseen the reality of executive ascendancy where governmental power is turned outward against the outside world for the security of our society. "The President," he declared in a noted debate in the House of Representatives before his elevation to the Chief Justiceship, "is the sole organ of the nation in its external relations. . . . He possesses the whole executive power. He holds and directs the force of the nation."

The full import of Marshall's dictum did not become apparent until the rise of the nation to a position of world leadership. If we look only to the intent of the Framers, the Constitution appears to contemplate a division of powers in the external field comparable to that provided for in domestic affairs. Throughout, the concept is that of power in the executive, with the legislature as a check—of the President as motor and the Congress as brake.

At the same time, in the world of the twentieth century, it is *power,* in the field of foreign affairs, that has waxed and *control* that has waned. The most important factor in American foreign policy in our day has been presidential leadership; the congressional check has at times seemed a mere shadow of that intended by the Framers. The reason for this is not difficult to perceive. "The initiative in foreign affairs," in Wilson's own words, "which the President possesses without any restriction whatever, is virtually the power to control them absolutely." In the field of external relations especially, the President *is* power. He has power of knowledge, will, and force. His decisions, applied through all the agents and material instruments at the command of the executive department, can set in motion actions that drastically affect every aspect of external relations—nay, even the very life of the Republic. The constitutional intent may be that, in this area, the President only *proposes,* while the Senate and Congress *dispose.* The power of initiative in foreign policy is, however, the power so to commit the nation that the congressional check may become only a formality.

What this means in practical terms was shown by what happened after the outbreak of the second great European conflict—particularly after the fall of France in 1940. That period has aptly been denominated, so far as the United States was concerned, "the War before the War." During it, the position of the nation in relation to the conflict was converted, largely on the initiative of the President, from that of a neutral to that of limited participant in the war. This occurred despite the fact that, during most of the period in question, the Neutrality Act of 1939, brought into operation by presidential proclamations of neutrality at the outset of the war, remained technically in force.

The first important executive measures in the direction of American participation in the conflict occurred after the fall of France. In September, 1940, an executive agreement was concluded transferring to Britain fifty destroyers in return for the lease of certain sites for naval bases in the Western Hemisphere. This action, taken solely on the authority of the President, involved participation by the United States in the European war. It constituted an American contribution designed to aid the cause of one of the belligerents in the conflict against its enemy.

Nor can the military value of such contribution, in the circumstances in which Britain then found herself, be denied. From the point of view of international law, the American action was inconsistent with the rules of neutrality as they had crystallized in the nineteenth century and the Hague Conventions. As Winston Churchill himself has conceded, "The transfer to Great Britain of fifty American warships was a decidedly unneutral act by the United States . . . . it was the first of a long succession of unneutral acts in the Atlantic which were of the utmost service to us. It marked the passage of the United States from being neutral to being nonbelligerent."

This is not to say that the action of the United States in this respect was a violation of the law of nations. On the contrary, it was amply justified by recognized canons of international law. The United States could properly invoke the right of self-defense against the overwhelming danger facing it, as well as all other countries, from the denial of the very bases of international law by nations bent on world domination. In the words of Secretary of State Cordell Hull: "assistance to those who resist attack is a vital part of our national self-defense. In the face of the forces of conquest now on the march across the world, self-defense is and must be the compelling consideration."

At the same time, the important thing for purposes of the present discussion is not the fact that the destroyer transfer was eminently justified, but that it did make the nation a participant in the European conflict. The President, on his own authority, was thus able to intervene in an existing war and convert the status of the United States from that of neutral to that of limited belligerent. If nothing else, the President's action constituted an announcement by the nation that it would no longer be bound by the normal international obligations resting upon neutrals.

In the year and some months which followed before Pearl Harbor, President Roosevelt acted directly to uphold the British cause by various military measures. The most important of them involved action taken to insure the adequate deliveries of war materials and other needed supplies to Britain. The President's action in this respect is of particular constitutional interest because of an express provision in the Lend-Lease Act of 1941, that "Nothing in this Act shall be construed to authorize or permit the authorization of convoying vessels by naval vessels of the United States."

On May 27, 1941, only two months after this provision was enacted, the President announced that American patrols were helping to insure the delivery of needed supplies to Britain. On July 7, the President informed Congress that he had concluded an agreement under which the United States would take over from Britain the defense of Iceland. On the same date, he stated that the Navy had been ordered to convoy supplies for Britain as far as Iceland. The American actions led to German attacks on the convoying vessels, which led, in turn, to the announcement, on September 11, by the President, that thenceforth Axis vessels entering "American defensive areas" would do so "at their peril" and that American naval forces had received orders to strike first at German and Italian submarines and surface vessels in such areas. On October 8, orders were issued to American naval forces in the Atlantic to fire at sight upon any Axis vessels or aircraft encountered.

In its declaration of war of December 11, 1941, Germany accused the United States of "having violated in the most flagrant manner . . . all rules of neutrality." This charge was, however, inconsistent with the facts insofar as the status of the United States in relation to the war was concerned. By the end of 1941, the position of this country could hardly be characterized as that of a neutral. Ever since the action of the President in transferring the destroyers to Britain, the nation had been a participant in the conflict. Soon after the destroyer deal, the United States was characterized as in a state of limited war. This may have been too extreme in 1940, but it was certainly accurate a year later. The President's order of September 11, 1941, created a state of hostilities in many respects indistinguishable from war. From that time onward, at the least, there was naval warfare between the United States and Germany.

The experience prior to the formal entry of the United States in the Second World War notably demonstrates the power of the President to intervene on behalf of a belligerent in a war to which the nation is not a declared party. It is true that, if one looks at the steps taken during the pre-Pearl Harbor period, it was not the President alone who acted in a manner inconsistent with the canons of neutrality. The Chief Executive was amply supported by the bulk of the country and the Congress. The action of the legislature was especially significant in its wholesale delegation of the authority to extend aid to Britain in the Lend-Lease Act. But the fact remains that presidential initiative was the dominant factor in changing the status of the nation from that of neutrality to that of active intervention in favor of Britain. It was the President who, notwithstanding the express congressional refusal to authorize it in the already-cited section of the Lend-Lease Act, ordered convoying—which, pushed gradually farther and farther across the Atlantic, resulted in the end in a shooting war, without Congress having been formally consulted.

The experience prior to Pearl Harbor indicates how the presidential power to direct the force of the nation has placed the constitutional authority to declare war in the shade. The unwritten constitutional law of presidential power (if not the text of the basic document) has all but vested in the highest officer the virtual authority to make war whenever deemed necessary to protect the interests of the United States. The nation has, in actual fact, been at war more often without, than with, an express declaration by the Congress. Indeed, even if we look to the wars waged with formal declarations, we find that, except perhaps for the Spanish-American War and, to a lesser extent, the War of 1812, the formal declarations merely confirmed states of war which had already been entered into, largely upon the initiative of the President.

With the attack on Pearl Harbor and the resulting congressional declarations of war, the position of the United States as a participant in the global conflict was, of course, wholly clarified. With the nation formally at war, the controversy between the partisans of intervention and isolation was stilled. The basic question then became that of how best to harness our resources for the needs of global conflict.

Total mobilization of both manpower and the economy reached its peak (in our system at least) during World War II. The authority exercised by the Federal Government under the war power was so vast that its extent can be but briefly sketched. The President was given the power by the Selective Training and Service Act to make rules and regulations for the drafting of male citizens into the armed forces, and to terminate their periods of service. So-called "conscription of industry" was also provided for: Plants that refused to give preference to the United States in the execution of war orders or to manufacture necessary supplies or to furnish them at a reasonable price as determined by the Secretary of War or the Navy could be taken over by the President.

In addition, broad requisitioning and priorities powers were conferred upon the President. He was authorized to requisition any property, equipment, machinery, tools, or supplies when he deemed such requisitioning was needed for the national defense. He could also, in his discretion, give priority over all deliveries for private account or for export to contracts or orders of the armed forces and all other contracts or orders which he deemed necessary or appropriate to promote the national defense. The President was also given the power to allocate any materials and facilities where necessary to the war effort. This power furnished the foundation for the extensive system of consumer rationing administered by the Office of Price Administration, as well as for the comprehensive control of industrial materials and output which was exercised by the War Production Board.

The broadest powers of price control and wage stabilization were likewise conferred. The Emergency Price Control Act of 1942 granted the power to regulate prices and rents in the most sweeping terms, and the Stabilization Act of the same year was similarly broad in its delegation of the authority to stabilize wages. Control of labor disputes affecting the war effort was provided for by the War Labor Disputes Act of 1943. The National War Labor Board was empowered to decide such labor disputes, and to provide by order the wages and hours and all other terms and conditions governing the relations between the parties. And, to enable the board's orders to be enforced, the President was empowered to commandeer plants whose operations were impaired by labor disturbances.

Under these and other war statutes delegating authority to him, President Franklin D. Roosevelt was vested with well-nigh complete power over person and property. But such total power in the Executive was deemed necessary to meet the demands of global war. And the Supreme Court was in the forefront of those recognizing this necessity. The power fully to mobilize manpower had been recognized in the government during the First World War; thus, as the high Court put it in 1948, "The constitutionality of the conscription of manpower for military service is beyond question." The Court's decisions arising out of World War II recognized in the government authority over property rights as extensive as that possessed by it over manpower. Said the Court, in the case just quoted from, with regard to the impact of "total global warfare" upon our system: "With the advent of such warfare, mobilized property in the form of equipment and supplies became as essential as mobilized manpower. Mobilization of effort extended not only to the uniformed armed services but to the entire population. . . . The language of the Constitution authorizing such measures is broad rather than restrictive."

Under the Constitution, the Congress is given the power "to raise and support Armies," "to provide and maintain a Navy," and to make all laws necessary and proper to carry these powers into execution. Under this authority, as we have already noted, the Congress can clearly draft men for battle service. And, according to a 1942 opinion of the high tribunal, "Its power to draft business organizations to support the fighting men who risk their lives can be no less."

During World War II also, there were dramatic conflicts between war and law comparable to those personified in 1861 by President Lincoln and Chief Justice Taney. Such conflict has rarely, if ever, taken place in a more dramatic setting than the Supreme Court building July 29–31, 1942. For it was on those days that the high tribunal heard and decided the case of the eight German saboteurs who had landed on our shores from submarines in June, 1942. The eight had been arrested by FBI agents soon after their landings and tried by a military commission specially appointed by President Roosevelt for offenses against the law of war and the Articles of War. The commission had found them guilty of violating the law of war by attempting sabotage of our war facilities and had ordered death sentences for six of them and prison terms for the other two.

The officers who had been appointed to defend the Germans before the military tribunal then sought *habeas corpus,* first from a district court, then from the Federal Court of Appeals in Washington, and then from the Supreme Court. To deal with the case "without any avoidable delay," the Court convened in July in Special Term, pursuant to a call to the vacationing Justices from Chief Justice Stone. It was during this special three-day session that the legality of the saboteurs' convictions was argued and determined, though the formal opinion of the Court, explaining its brief July 31 announcement that the military trial had been valid, was not filed until three months later, weeks after the death sentences ordered by the military commission had been carried out.

The judicial role in the case of the German saboteurs differs strikingly from that in the *Merryman* case of almost a century earlier where Chief Justice Taney eloquently, though unavailingly, asserted the illegality of military detentions. In 1861 (as we saw in Chapter V) the military declined obedience to a writ of *habeas corpus* issued by Taney upon the ground that the writ had been "suspended." In 1942, too, the President sought to insulate the military arrest and conviction from judicial control. The President's proclamation appointing the military commission and directing it to try the saboteurs provided expressly that the Germans were not to be permitted "to seek any remedy or maintain any proceeding directly or indirectly, or to have any such remedy or proceeding sought on their behalf, in the courts." But this part of the proclamation was quietly ignored, the high Court stating only "neither the Proclamation nor the fact that they are enemy aliens forecloses consideration by the courts of petitioners' contentions that the Constitution and laws of the United States constitutionally enacted forbid their trial by military commission." The saboteurs were thus given a full judicial hearing on the legality of their convictions, despite the President's attempt completely to bar the courts from the case.

Yet, if the judges were thus able, in the case of the German saboteurs, to vindicate the supremacy of law in the face of an executive *ipse dixit,* that did not end the conflict between law and military power during World War II. A striking clash occurred in Hawaii, where martial law had been proclaimed just after Pearl Harbor. In July, 1943, two naturalized Germans, who had been held in custody in Hawaii by the military (one since December, 1941, and the other since December, 1942), filed petitions for *habeas corpus.* The district judge ruled that, since there was no showing that the territory was any longer in danger of invasion, the writ should issue.

There then ensued a conflict between the law and the military reminiscent of that which took place when Chief Justice Taney issued the writ in the *Merryman* case. The Commanding General in Hawaii refused to obey the writ and was cited for contempt and fined $5,000 ($4,000 more than Andrew Jackson for his celebrated contempt just after the battle of New Orleans). The general countered with an order forbidding any judge in the territory to entertain a petition for *habeas corpus* and directing the district judge by name to stay and desist from further proceedings in the instant case, on pain of a penalty of fine or imprisonment to be imposed by a military tribunal. Here was a defiance of the law by the military as flagrant as any in American history. This time, however, it was the military authorities who gave way. The Commanding General rescinded his order and the two prisoners were released. The district judge refused to expunge the contempt judgment, though he did reduce the fine to $100 (and that amount was ultimately remitted through a presidential pardon).

Perhaps the greatest failure of American law during World War II may be illustrated by the case of Toyosaburo Korematsu. As graphically described in 1944 by a member of the highest bench, his case is one that is unique in our system:

> Korematsu was born on our soil, of parents born in Japan. The Constitution makes him a citizen of the United States by nativity and a citizen of California by residence. No claim is made that he is not loyal to this country. There is no suggestion that apart from the matter involved here he is not law-abiding and well disposed. Korematsu, however, has been convicted of an act not commonly a crime. It consists merely of being present in the state whereof he is a citizen, near the place where he was born, and where all his life he has lived.

Had Korematsu been of Italian, German, or English ancestry, his act would not have been a crime. His presence in California was made a crime solely because his parents were of Japanese birth. The difference between innocence and crime, so far as he was concerned, resulted not from anything he did, said, or even thought, but only from his particular racial stock. For Korematsu was a victim of what a *Harper's* article was to term "America's Greatest Wartime Mistake," namely, the evacuation of those of Japanese ancestry from the West Coast shortly after the Pearl Harbor attack.

Acting upon their belief that those of Japanese ancestry posed a security threat after Pearl Harbor, the military moved to eliminate the danger by a number of restrictive measures. The most important of them were a series of Civilian Exclusion Orders, issued early in 1942, excluding "all persons of Japanese ancestry, both alien and non-alien" from the westernmost part of the country. Those so excluded were gathered together in so-called "assembly centers" and then evacuated to what were euphemistically termed "relocation centers" in interior states, where they were detained until almost the end of the war. Under this evacuation program, over 112,000 persons of Japanese ancestry were herded from their homes on the West Coast into the relocation centers, which, had they been set up in any other country, we would not hesitate to call by their true name of concentration camps.

The record of his government in dealing with the West-Coast Japanese during the war is hardly one which an American can contemplate with satisfaction. As the high Court eloquently declared in 1943, "Distinctions between citizens solely because of their ancestry are by their very nature odious to a free people whose institutions are founded upon the doctrine of equality." Yet it cannot be gainsaid that those who, like Toyosaburo Korematsu, were forced into the relocation centers were deprived of their freedom merely because they were the children of parents they had not chosen and belonged to a race from which there was no way to resign.

It is true that the Supreme Court did, in December, 1944, order the release of the Japanese-Americans from the relocation centers, on the ground that, though the original evacuations might have been justified by necessity, such necessity did not exist three years after Pearl Harbor, during which time the government had ample opportunity to separate the loyal from the disloyal among those detained.

Yet the *Endo* case, in which such release was ordered, shows clearly the practical limitations of judicial control as a check on military arbitrariness. Mitsuye Endo was evacuated from her home and placed in a relocation center early in 1942. In July, 1942, she filed a petition for a writ of *habeas corpus* in a federal district court; it was not until December, 1944, that she was ordered released by the Supreme Court. But the Court's decision did not and could not affect her three-year deprivation of liberty, illegal though the deprivation might have been. Despite the Supreme Court's decision, to quote from the concurring opinion of Justice Owen J. Roberts, "An admittedly loyal citizen has been deprived of her liberty for a period of years. Under the Constitution she should be free to come and go as she pleases. Instead, her liberty of motion and other innocent activities have been prohibited and conditioned."

This is not, of course, to deny the importance of judicial

control in our system. Such control serves both to restrain improper exercises of authority and to correct abuses after they have arisen. In particular cases, it may even be the restraining aspect that is the more significant. To those affected, Supreme Court reversal of arbitrary action can never be as satisfactory as proper action in the first place would have been. Mitsuye Endo may have the satisfaction of being enshrined in the *Supreme Court Reports;* but she is most unlikely to consider that an adequate substitute for her loss of liberty during her illegal confinement in the relocation center.

When World War II ended, it was apparent that Hughes's dire prediction (referred to at the outset of the chapter) had not materialized. Once again, the American constitutional system survived despite the forebodings of one of its most eminent sons. Yet, if the basic structure emerged from the second global conflict essentially unimpaired, it can hardly be denied that the war left as its legal heritage a vital shift in the constitutional balance of power.

The postwar period has seen an essential continuation of the presidential primacy that was the principal characteristic of the American polity during the war itself. In large part, this has been a direct result of the nature of the postwar world. If, as already seen, the period before Pearl Harbor may be denominated "the War before the War," that since the surrender of Germany and Japan may be termed "the Peace without true Peace." The period has been passed in a twilight zone between war and peace —in a penumbra labeled "cold war." In the striking phrase of the highest Court, this has been a time "when the guns are silent, but the peace of Peace has not come."

In an era of cold war, as in one of formal conflict, national leadership inevitably gravitates to that department which commands the force of the society. This has been particularly true insofar as the performance of the nation's vital role as leader of the free-world community has been concerned.

As is well known, the constitutional requirement of senatorial consent to treaties by a two-thirds vote prevented American participation after World War I in the effort to preserve the peace through international collective action. The post-1918 experience in this respect was not repeated after the second global conflict. Having learned, in Franklin Roosevelt's phrase, that, "when peace has been broken anywhere, the peace of all countries everywhere is in danger," the nation has come, since World War II, to be the prime mover in an elaborate system of collective security, set up under agreements between ourselves and other countries or international organizations. These have ranged from bilateral treaties, to multilateral treaties of a regional character (such as that establishing the North Atlantic Treaty Organization), to the United Nations Charter.

As a practical matter, implementation of the commitments assumed by the nation under the collective-security arrangements entered into by it since World War II has rested almost entirely in the discretion of the executive department. The President has determined whether and how to deploy and employ the armed forces to perform the collective-security obligations of the nation. This has been true even when presidential action in this respect has been met by force (thus virtually embroiling the nation in war).

The reality of presidential power in this respect is shown by what happened when the United States was first called upon to fulfill its commitment under the United Nations Charter to provide force to enable the world organization to deal with armed aggression. On June 25, 1950, South Korea was invaded by North Korean forces. Twenty-four hours later, the United Nations Security Council passed a resolution which determined that the attack was a breach of international peace, called for the withdrawal of the invading troops, and requested member nations to "give every assistance to the United Nations" in coping with the situation. The aggression, nevertheless, moved ahead rapidly and, on June 27, President Truman ordered United States air and sea forces to aid the South Korean troops. The President stated that he had done so in order to support the Security Council resolution. Shortly thereafter, American land forces in substantial numbers were sent in at the President's direction to help repel the North Korean invasion.

What was the legal situation when President Truman thus

ordered the use of the armed forces in compliance with the Security Council's request for assistance? It was the President, acting on his own authority, who ordered American forces to intervene. His action in this respect was not seriously challenged, on constitutional grounds, in either the Congress or the country. Nor is it seen how the legal authority of the President to act as he did could seriously be disputed. The President may direct the use of force to protect American interests abroad and may supply the force needed to fulfill the collective-security obligations of the nation. "Prompt action was imperative," said President Truman, in explaining his action to Congress almost a month after he had moved. In such a case, the President must be able to act immediately, without any obligation to seek legislative approval.

The Korean action taken by President Truman demonstrates beyond doubt the presidential power to take whatever action (including use of the armed forces) he deems necessary to fulfill the international obligations of the nation. The reality of the postwar world—if not the strict letter of the Constitution—has made presidential primacy in the international field a compelling necessity, even if that has meant the taking of belligerent action without congressional consent. This has been true under all our postwar Presidents. The Truman action in Korea has its counterparts in the 1958 intervention in Lebanon by Eisenhower and the 1962 confrontation over Cuba under Kennedy. In those cases also the President directed the use of the armed forces—though, in both, such use was happily not met by any opposing force.

In our internal affairs, too, the tensions of the cold-war period have had important constitutional effects. We are perhaps too close to some of the excesses committed during the period to be able to speak impartially of it. These excesses did, however, teach us that security, like the patriotism of which Dr. Johnson speaks, might also come to be the last refuge of a scoundrel; many have been the things done in security's name in a time of tension that would not be tolerated at other times.

The basic problem of a legal system like ours is that of reconciling the antinomy between liberty and security. Both have, to be sure, always been essential elements in the polity, whose co-existence has had to be reconciled by the law. In the postwar period, nevertheless, it has been the element of security that has tended to dominate. The response of our government to the tensions of the cold war has made our law security-conscious as it has never before been in our history.

The governmental demand for security has been articulated in important laws and other measures restricting rights formerly deemed fundamental. For the first time since the notorious Alien and Sedition Laws themselves, a peacetime sedition law (making subversive speech alone criminal) was used to put people in prison. The law in question—the Smith Act—was enacted in 1940; but the first significant prosecutions, those brought in 1948 against the leaders of the American Communist Party, were a direct fruit of the postwar confrontation between the Western world and the Soviet Union.

In addition, other significant restrictions were imposed upon Communists in this country—ranging from drastic restraints upon aliens to the requirement of registration as subversives. Even more extreme has been the Internal Security Act of 1950, which provides for the detention by the executive branch, during specified emergencies, without warrant or judicial hearing, of subversives and others deemed to present any security dangers. Such a law (the first in our history vesting in the President wholesale powers of arrest and detention) stands in stark contrast to the attitude of Woodrow Wilson, when he opposed a similar bill in 1917. "I think," declared Wilson then, "that it is not only unconstitutional, but in its character would put us upon the level of the very people we are fighting."

In their effect upon the community, the security measures that have had the greatest impact have been the different loyalty programs instituted by governments in this country. At its peak, the federal program alone covered some six million civilian employees in both government and private industry; and this figure did not include the millions affected by comparable measures in the states.

It is now felt that much of the governmental reaction to the cold war went to unnecessary extremes: for a molehill of security, a mountain of undesirable security apparatus was built up. The loyalty-security programs, in particular, have caused widespread uneasiness. During the first century and a half of the Republic, our people took it for granted that those whom they employed as government servants were loyal to the United States. So far as their loyalty was concerned, civil servants were asked only to take the oath to support and defend our Constitution. More recently, it was urged that this was hardly enough to insure the loyalty of government employees. Yet, paradoxically enough, has not this concern over loyalty itself been an indication that loyalty in this country has not been what it was in former days? While the Decii are rushing with devoted bodies on the enemies of Rome, what need is there of preaching patriotism? When loyalty is made a principal object of the nation's concern, it has already sunk from its pristine all-transcendent condition.

A natural question which arises in a constitutional system such as ours is whether the restrictive measures adopted during the cold war could be reconciled with the demands of the Bill of Rights, particularly the First Amendment. The legislative measures already referred to were all upheld by the Supreme Court (except for the preventive detention provisions of the Internal Security Act, which fortunately have not as yet had the occasion to come into operation).

In the most important cases, the prosecution of Communists under the Smith Act was sustained because of the "clear and present danger" presented by Communist advocacy during the tensions of the postwar period; the restrictions on Communist aliens were ruled within the plenary power of Congress over citizens of other lands; and the federal loyalty program was upheld under the "settled principle that government employment . . . can be revoked at the will of the appointing officer." In addition, the high bench refused to strike down restrictions upon the procedural rights of notice and full hearing in cases where national security was involved.

The decisions referred to, which occurred during the first part of the cold-war period (before the accession of Earl Warren to the Chief Justiceship) may be understandable as a continued reaction from the excesses of judicial supremacy in the pre-1937 period. The judges who had repudiated those excesses in the constitutional revolution discussed in the last chapter not unnaturally continued to display the same Holmesian approach of deference to the legislator during the period under discussion.

One may wonder, nevertheless, whether the high bench did not go too far in standing aside while (as Robert G. McCloskey expresses it) the winds howled on Capitol Hill and elsewhere. It is a common saying among lawyers that hard cases make bad law. What is not so generally realized is that cases decided under severe stress may make equally bad law. A Court overimbued with the dominant demand for security may tend to give effect to that demand, even if the cost be some distortion of accepted principles of constitutional law. Yet this can hardly be done without important effects upon the general jurisprudence of that Court.

A tribunal that molds its law only to fit the immediate demands of public sentiment is hardly fulfilling the role proper to the supreme bench in a system such as ours. As Justice Frankfurter once put it, "The Court has no reason for existence if it merely reflects the pressures of the day." Of course, the judges should act in this field in a manner consistent with the doctrine of deference to the legislature that has dominated its work since 1937. But abnegation on the part of the Court hardly requires abdication by it of the judicial function. Certainly, whatever may be said about the strains and stresses of the cold-war period, the enemy has not yet been so near the gates that we must abandon our respect for the organic traditions that have heretofore prevailed in our system.

XI

THE CONTEMPORARY CONSTITUTION

THE LAW, says Cardozo in a famous passage, has its epochs of ebb and flow. This has certainly been true insofar as American constitutional law has been concerned. Indeed, if we look at the governmental structure set up by the Framers, our constitutional development is seen to be largely a record of ebbs and flows. During the first part of the Republic's development—extending from its founding to the end of Reconstruction—the paramount theme in the polity was that of legislative primacy. During the next period—from roughly 1890 to the Second Administration of Franklin D. Roosevelt—the system was dominated by judicial supremacy. The third period—from the constitutional revolution of 1937 to the present—has been essentially one of presidential preponderance.

The last thirty years without a doubt have seen a continuing augmentation in the power of the President. The exigencies of economic crisis, global conflict, and the cold war—these have all been met by assertions of executive authority. Our generation has, in effect, been witnessing the latest in the historic shifts that have occurred in the constitutional structure.

In the preceding chapter, we emphasized the paramount position of the President in the conduct of the nation's external relations—whether during war or a time of formal peace. Since

Franklin Roosevelt's day, the Chief Executive has all but had the field of foreign affairs to himself. "In this vast external realm," the Supreme Court itself declared in 1936, "with its important, complicated, delicate and manifold problems, the President alone has the power to speak or listen as a representative of the nation." Into that field "the Senate cannot intrude and Congress itself is powerless to invade it." The power to direct the force of the nation, we saw, permits the highest officer to take action, such as the decision of President Truman to intervene in Korea, which leaves the Congress and the country no alternative but to follow the lead which he has given.

It is, however, inaccurate to assume that presidential primacy at the present time is limited to the field of foreign affairs. On the contrary, from the accession of Franklin Roosevelt to the Presidency, executive leadership has permeated well-nigh every aspect of the governmental structure. The fulcrum of the American polity has moved ever more steadily from Capitol Hill to the other end of Pennsylvania Avenue.

Wherever we look in the American system today, we are met by the reality of presidential authority. There is inherent in the highest office power and prestige that few in government are able to withstand. This is true even insofar as the members of the legislative department are concerned. In drama, magnitude, and prestige, the President so far overshadows all others that almost alone he fills the public eye and ear. No one else can begin to compete with him in access to the public mind through modern methods of communications.

The national forum is one which is always available to a President who seeks to secure popular support for his program. The great Presidents of this century, Franklin Roosevelt has said, were "moral leaders, each in his own way and for his own time, who used the Presidency as a pulpit." In many ways, in fact, the test of the modern President is his ability to muster public opinion behind his program. The President can always counter opposition in the Congress by taking his case directly to the people. Describing his conflicts with congressional leaders, Theodore Roosevelt writes: "I was forced to abandon the effort to persuade them to come my way, and then I achieved results only by appealing over the heads of the Senate and House leaders to the people, who were the masters of both of us."

Today, the effective use of television and radio—which gives the President the entire nation for an audience—offers him the certainty that his case will be heard as he presents it. If the President can marshal public opinion behind his program, it is a hardy Congress which can resist its enactment into law. The real source of the President's power, it has been well stated, lies ultimately in the appeal to public opinion.

From what has been said, it is obvious that modern Presidents have repudiated the sense of the so-called Wade-Davis Manifesto of 1864, that the duty of the President is only to obey and execute, not to take any part in making, the laws. The President feels the need to lead, in the Congress, as in the nation. The Constitution bids him speak, and times of stress and change have more and more thrust upon him the role of originator in the legislative process. In legislation, as in other areas, his is the vital place of action in the system.

In this respect, of particular significance has been the emergence of the President as a force in the origination and formulation of legislation. Our day has witnessed a tremendous rise of presidential power in initiating legislation and expediting its progress through the Congress. There has been a growing tendency for major laws to originate in the executive departments. As problems of lawmaking have become ever more technical, the Congress has turned increasingly to the Executive for guidance in drafting laws. Thus, it has been estimated that fully four out of five laws of any importance passed during Franklin Roosevelt's First Administration originated in the White House or in the executive departments. The habit then formed has persisted in more recent administrations.

The role of the President as shaper of legislation has, without doubt, been inevitable, in view of the technical skills and continuous services of the executive branch at his disposal, which the Congress is hardly equipped to match. The constitutional picture of the President remains, it is true, only that of a chief magistrate, whose sole duty in the area of lawmaking is to recommend those measures which he deems expedient. With that, he leaves the matter, and the responsibility is now with the legislative power.

How different has the reality become from this picture! The President and his Cabinet have all too often tended to regard themselves as the real legislative department, with the Congress expected to receive and act upon their views. It is, indeed, a far cry from the attitude of the Senate in 1908, when a furor was created because a member of the Cabinet sent to that body the complete draft of a proposed bill. Today, the drafting of legislation by the executive departments has become a commonplace.

The unfolding of the Presidency in our own day has, without a doubt, made poor prophets of those in the Framers' convention who feared that the Executive would inevitably be reduced by the legislature to the mere pageant and shadow of magistracy. On the contrary, if there is one thing that disturbs present-day students of the American polity, it is the deterioration that has occurred in the position of the legislative department. It may, indeed, be said that, as the global responsibilities of the nation have increased, the power and prestige of the Congress have correspondingly declined.

Leaving aside the grosser manifestations of congressional decay —the diminution in the caliber of legislative personnel, the venality and conflicts of interest that permeate Capitol Hill, the common attitude reflected in the congressman as a staple butt of popular humor—one has only to look at the manner in which the Congress functions to realize its manifest inadequacy for the needs of the mid-twentieth century.

"How," asks Dr. Ernest S. Griffith, Director of the Legislative Reference Service, "can a group of nonspecialists, elected as representatives of the electorate, really function in a specialized and technological age?" This question is certainly one of the most difficult placed before the contemporary representative democracy. But it is one that the American legislature has not even begun to answer. The congressional mode of operation is scarcely one to give confidence to those who believe in representative government and seek to preserve it as a flourishing institution even in an atomic age.

Congress, it has aptly been said, is alone among all private or governmental bodies charged with any kind of responsibility which lets leadership depend exclusively upon the accident of tenure. "Under this system," Senator Kefauver tells us, "the member of the party in power who has served the longest in any given committee is for practical purposes the *only* person eligible for the chairmanship of that committee regardless of his qualifications, physical fitness, or any other factor that might be weighed, or any other method of trying to pick the best person for the post."

One who works in or with the Congress soon finds that that institution is not so much a coherent governmental organ as a series of fragmented individual power bases. In this respect, the senior members of the two houses may be compared to a group of feudal chieftains. The chairmen of major committees each have their own baronial fiefs—tied together by often vague allegiance to party and its chief, but dominated most of all by desire to conserve the power and perquisites pertaining to each particular barony.

The comparison just suggested is most disquieting to one who contemplates the future constitutional development of the American Republic. An institution dominated by feudal characteristics can scarcely prove equal to the needs of the mid-twentieth-century world. More than that, such an institution is, if it remains unchanged, bound to suffer the fate of all anachronistic survivals in a rapidly changing society. In too many ways, today's Congress seems comparable to the feudal lords of an earlier day, vainly seeking to hold back the surge of a royal power whose triumph had been rendered inevitable by the time's necessities.

The principles of a free constitution, says Gibbon, are irrevocably lost when the independence of the legislature is destroyed. Certainly, the history of that people with whom his name is forever associated amply demonstrates the truth of such observation. One may go further and state that, from the Roman Republic of old to the Fourth French Republic of our own day, decline of the legislative department has been the harbinger of the decay of republican institutions themselves. An observer of the congressional onrush toward its nadir may well wonder whether it alone will avoid the history of similar assemblies which have brought ruin upon the State or sunk under the burden of their own imbecility.

When we turn to the third great department in the contemporary constitutional structure—that branch which is naturally of the utmost importance to the development of our basic document—the picture is not so clear-cut. It is erroneous to assume, as all too many commentators do, that constitutional history must unfold in a strictly consistent evolution—with the dominant theme of any particular period inexorably determining every aspect of its organic unfolding.

A picture of constitutional history in terms of a completely consistent development is bound to be oversimplified and somewhat distorted. Of course, if we analyze the characteristics of any period in the nation's history, we will find a basic stream, dominated by the primacy, as already stated, of one of the three departments. Within it, however, we will note inconsistent currents, at variance with, and even at cross-purposes to, the underlying drift of the stream.

What has just been said may be well illustrated by the role of the Supreme Court during the present period of American constitutional history. The last two chapters have shown dramatically the lesser part played by the high bench in the post-1937 organic structure. One who was familiar with the augmented position assumed by the Court during the heyday of judicial supremacy, and the complete repudiation of such position in the cases discussed in Chapter IX, might, not unnaturally, have concluded that judicial, like legislative, decline was to be an essential characteristic of the next period of our constitutional history.

Such conclusion is bound to be reinforced by the basically subdued role played by the highest tribunal during World War II and the early postwar years. The decisions placing the judicial imprimatur upon the most extreme governmental measures of the first part of the cold war period seem also to illustrate how the flow of executive authority has been accompanied by a correlative ebb in judicial power.

The developments discussed in the last two chapters led many, in C. Herman Pritchett's phrase, to expect the Supreme Court to wither away, much as the State was supposed to do in Marxist theory. Yet, if one thing is clear, it is that both the Soviet State and our high tribunal have anything but withered away in recent years. The Supreme Court has been as much in the headlines and the center of controversy during the past decade as it has ever been, and while this may hardly be a true criterion of its effectiveness, it surely shows the continued significance of the Court in the constitutional scheme of things.

It is true that the work of the high bench today is different than it was in the pre-1937 period. If, in 1922, a federal judge could assert "that of the three fundamental principles which underlie government, and for which government exists, the protection of life, liberty, and property, the chief of these is property," the judicial emphasis in our own day has surely shifted in favor of the other two. While most of the work of the pre-1937 Supreme Court concerned the protection of *property* rights against what were conceived as governmental violations of due process, in the present Court the judicial concern has focused upon *personal* rights. It may, indeed, be said that the primary role played by the high bench today is as guardian of civil liberties.

In 1886, as discerning an observer as Sir Henry Maine could refer to our Bill of Rights as "a certain number of amendments on comparatively unimportant points." Today, such an observation could scarcely be made by anyone the least conversant with American constitutional law. On the contrary, the Bill of Rights, and the post-Civil War amendments, making its basic safeguards binding upon the states as well, have become the very stuff of which our constitutional law is now made.

In enforcing the civil liberties guaranteed by the basic document, the Supreme Court has forged for itself a new and vital place in the constitutional structure. More and more (at least in cases which do not involve seditious or subversive activities), the high tribunal has come to display its solicitude for the personal rights of the individual. Freedom of speech, press, religion, the rights of minorities and those accused of crime, those of individuals subjected to legislative and administrative inquisitions—all have, in recent years, come under the fostering guardianship of the highest bench.

Perhaps the most important work done by the Supreme Court in the field of civil liberties has been its protection of the rights of minorities. "The most certain test," says Lord Acton, "by which we judge whether a country is really free is the amount of security enjoyed by minorities." From this point of view, the situation in much of the United States not too long ago was far from encouraging. Despite the intent of their framers, the post-bellum amendments were all but read out of the basic document, so far as ameliorating the legal position of the Negro was concerned.

It is in our own day that the changed attitude of the Supreme Court to the protection of personal rights has made equal protection and due process more than mere slogans for minority groups. Particularly with regard to racial discriminations, there has been a complete alteration in the judicial attitude. For virtually the first time since their adoption, the gulf between the letter of the Fourteenth and Fifteenth Amendments and their practical effect has been significantly narrowed.

In its decisions in recent years, the Supreme Court has removed the legal prop from the three most important manifestations of racial discrimination in this country. In an important 1944 case, the so-called "white primary" (upon which Southern efforts to disfranchise the Negro were based) was ruled unconstitutional. In 1948, the enforcement of racial restrictive covenants was stricken down. And then, in the 1954 case of *Brown v. Board of Education,* the enforced segregation upon which the whole pattern of Southern discrimination against the Negro has depended was held violative of the equal protection clause.

The *Brown* decision outlawing segregation in schools was as momentous as any ever rendered by a judicial tribunal. For, make no mistake about it, it will ultimately have an impact upon a whole community's way of life comparable to that caused by the most drastic political revolution or military conflict.

The road to the *Brown* decision was pointed to by the proviso of equality laid down in the 1896 case of *Plessy v. Ferguson* itself (Chapter VII), whose "separate but equal" doctrine has been the legal cornerstone of Southern segregation. Starting in 1937, the Supreme Court began to emphasize the requirement of equality in the separate facilities provided for the Negro in the field of education. The cases from 1937 to 1954 placed ever-increasing stress upon the judicial implementation of the requirement of equality in facilities. The Court's decisions tended toward the doctrine that, where higher education is concerned, separate facilities for the Negro are inherently unequal. From there, it was a short (though vital) step to the *Brown* decision itself.

What is true of segregation in higher education is also true of segregation as such. There can never be real equality in separated facilities, for the mere fact of segregation makes for discrimination. The arbitrary separation of the Negro, solely on the basis of race, is, in the phrase of the *Plessy* dissent, a "badge of servitude" and must generate in him a feeling of inferior social status, regardless of the formal equality of the facilities provided for him. And if that be the case, then, as the *Brown* decision ruled, segregation as such is discriminatory and hence a denial of the equal protection of the laws demanded by the Constitution.

As is well known, implementation of the *Brown* decision has seen the revival in our own day of controversy between state and federal power. The ghost of state sovereignty, which (one would have thought) had been laid to rest by Appomattox, has suddenly stirred from its deserved repose.

Shortly after the Supreme Court announced its decisions holding the segregation of Negroes in schools unconstitutional, so-called resolutions of "interposition" were adopted by the legislatures of several Southern states. That passed in Georgia in 1956 is typical of all of them and may be referred to for illustrative purposes. Expressly labeled a resolution "to invoke the doctrine of interposition," it asserts that the "decisions and orders of the Supreme Court of the United States relating to separation of the races in the public institutions of a State . . . are null, void and of no force or effect." In view of this, the resolution goes on, "There is declared the firm intention of this State to take all appropriate measures . . . to avoid this illegal encroachment upon the rights of her people."

As a matter of constitutional law, such state assertions of a right of interposition are no more valid than those stricken down so decisively in Marshall's and Taney's day. In the 1958 case of *Cooper v. Aaron,* the Supreme Court was presented directly with the claim that the Governor and legislature of Arkansas were not bound by the decision invalidating school segregation. This contention was disposed of in incisive terms. No principle, said the Court, is more firmly established in American public law than that binding the states to interpretations by the highest tribunal of the supreme law of the land. *Marbury v. Madison* (1803) "declared the basic principle that the federal judiciary is supreme in the exposition of the law of the Constitution, and that principle has ever since been respected by this Court and the Country as a permanent and indispensable feature of our constitutional system."

The conclusion is consequently clear that interposition is not a *constitutional* doctrine. At best, it is illegal defiance of constitutional authority. If the states can nullify federal action in the manner claimed by advocates of the interposition doctrine, the Constitution itself, declares the *Cooper v. Aaron* opinion (repeating a famous statement of Chief Justice Marshall), "becomes a solemn mockery."

From a strictly legal point of view, perhaps, *Cooper v. Aaron* may appear to constitute merely the hammering of additional nails into the coffin of dead constitutional doctrine. It is, nevertheless, essential that the law seize every opportunity to repudiate a doctrine so completely opposed to the fundamentals of the American constitutional system. To be sure, the essential tenet of the interposition doctrine denies the very authority of the Federal Supreme Court to make decisions binding on the states in such cases. "WHEREAS the States," categorically affirms the 1956 Alabama interposition resolution, "being the parties to the constitutional compact, it follows of necessity that there can be no tribunal above their authority to decide, in the last resort, whether the compact made by them be violated."

Thus to deny the authority of the highest Court in constitutional questions concerning the states is, in effect, to deny to our federalism the means of operating effectively. In Justice Frankfurter's words, "Compliance with decisions of this Court, as the constitutional organ of the supreme Law of the Land, has often, throughout our history, depended on active support by state and local authorities. It presupposes such support. To withhold it, and indeed to use political power to try to paralyze the supreme Law, precludes the maintenance of our federal system as we have known and cherished it for one hundred and seventy years."

The controversy over the high bench's desegregation decision and the judicial role in cases like *Cooper v. Aaron* (in maintaining the Constitution as the supreme law of the land) illustrates a second essential part played by the Supreme Court in the present period of our constitutional development—that of arbiter of the federal system. Such a role is of equal importance to that already discussed of guardian of civil liberties. If federalism is to work, an independent judicial tribunal must be its arbiter. "What is essential for federal government," to quote a leading English study, "is that some impartial body, independent of general and regional governments, should decide upon the meaning of the division of powers. . . . No alternative scheme with less inconveniences seems possible, consistently with maintaining the federal principle."

In our system, the role of arbiter is performed by the Supreme Court—in cases ranging from those involving state burdens upon interstate commerce to those arising from state infringements upon the supremacy clause. In this respect, the high bench is the bolt that holds the federal machinery together. Draw it out and there would be no real federal system, but only a moral union between the states.

To be sure, the Court's work in deciding controversies between state and federal power—and particularly its resolution of the desegregation question—have been criticized as primarily political in nature. Such criticism, however, ignores the essential nature of the highest bench in our constitutional system. Even those to whom the law is the most esoteric of mysteries should by now know that the Supreme Court makes decisions that are political as much as legal. We have endowed a judicial tribunal with the authority to decide disputes that, in other systems, are fought out at the political level.

In political impact, few decisions of the highest Court have had as great effect as that rendered in the 1962 case of *Baker v. Carr,* and none shows better that (as Paul Freund puts it), the predicted demise of the Supreme Court, like the report of Mark Twain's death, has been grossly exaggerated. In the *Baker* case, the Court held that it was within the competence of the federal courts to entertain an action challenging a statute apportioning legislative districts as contrary to the equal protection clause.

The result of *Baker v. Carr* is that the remedy for unfairness in districting is in the federal courts, as well as in the legislature itself. The ultimate consequence is bound to be elimination of much of the disproportionate influence which rural areas have had in choosing legislative personnel and a shifting of the legislative balance to those urban concentrations in which the bulk of Americans now live. Court-ordered reapportionment will more and more give urban and suburban areas a larger voice in state legislatures, and eventually in Congress.

The provocative possibility in such an outcome is that it may lead to the revitalization of the legislative department itself, a revitalization that is so urgently needed if the representative democracy provided by the Framers is to survive. Not so long ago, during the "court-packing" struggle of the mid-1930's, it was the Congress which preserved the Supreme Court as an effective judicial institution. Is it too fanciful to hope that, when all the ramifications of *Baker v. Carr* have been revealed, it will this time be the high bench that has come to the rescue of the legislative department and furnished the catalyst for sorely needed congressional rejuvenation?

The decisions protecting personal rights and safeguarding the federal system demonstrate how the Supreme Court has been able to fashion for itself a constitutional role adapted to today's needs. This role is vital in an age when the individual is in danger of being overwhelmed by concentrations of power. At the same time, it is altogether different from that played in the constitutional structure by the pre-1937 Court. If, indeed, the constitutional revolution of 1937 settled anything, it was what has been aptly termed the end of economic supervision by the judiciary. If, as seen in Chapter VIII, it was a relatively rare piece of regulatory legislation that was able to run the due process gantlet between 1890 and 1937, in the period since that time the due process clause itself has all but been removed as a substantive check upon governmental action in the economic sphere.

In the economic sphere, in truth, the drastic alteration in the high bench's jurisprudence has completely modified the nature of our constitutional law. More than that, it has been felt by many that this change is not one that is necessarily progressive in character. "The Constitution is gone," wailed Justice McReynolds from the bench at one of the decisions signaling the abandonment of judicial supremacy. To all too many, it has seemed that the free society of our fathers is also gone. To them, Maine's celebrated dictum on the progress from status to contract must be taken as a fundamental axiom which the society can violate only at the peril of social retrogression.

It should, however, be pointed out that most people today have come to realize that freedom of contract was pushed too far by the law of half a century ago. "Nothing, it has been said," declared a 1942 federal opinion, "exceeds like excess. Laissez-faire went too far." If unlimited freedom of contract alone is to prevail, the individual may, in practical reality, be forced to part, by the very contract which he is allowed to make, with all real freedom. Individualism, here as elsewhere, if utterly unrestrained, becomes self-devouring. It is no accident that Jeremy Bentham, very early in his career, bitterly assailed even the laws regulating usury as infringements upon freedom of trade in money-lending.

To one who takes for gospel the doctrine of progress from status to contract, the law of the mid-twentieth century may seem, in all too many ways, an indication of basic social retrogression. For the movement from status to contract, which had characterized our society since the decay of feudalism, has now been checked and even reversed. The modern expansion of the public-welfare concept has severely reduced the descriptive validity of Maine's maxim for our age.

In an earlier day, the government stood by, its main task to keep the ring while private interests asserted themselves freely. Just as in biology the physically stronger survive, so in law the economically stronger would prevail and survive. Our own day has seen the growth of an entirely different conception of the role of the legal order. The modern law has changed its purpose from the upholding of an abstract autonomy of the will to vindication of an active social concern in the protection of the economically weaker members of the society. Such change has been manifested in laws providing for workmen's compensation, the regulation of terms and conditions of contracts of employment, and the imposition on the employer and the community as a whole of the responsibility of caring for its less fortunate members, stricken by old age or unemployment—all of which have now been sustained by the Supreme Court.

Wherever we look in the law today, we find a growing importance of status, as opposed to contract—if we mean by status the attachment of legal consequences to the position of the individual concerned, irrespective of his volition in the matter. This means that legal liability is coming to result more and more from a given calling or situation—as employer, worker, landowner, insurer, consumer—rather than from the exercise of his free will by an independent individual.

Must we conclude from this that the present-day society, in thus reversing the order of social movement posited by Maine, has ceased to be a progressive society and is, indeed, returning to a concept of status reminiscent of the medieval law?

In the economic sphere, we do seem to be moving in the direction of a relationally organized society. The basic picture, as Roscoe Pound puts it, can no longer be one of wholly free competitive activity of economically autonomous individuals and units. It must be redrawn as one of the adjusted relations of economically interdependent individuals and units.

But this does not necessarily mean that the society is in a

state of retrogression merely because of its failure to conform to the gospel of social progress according to Sir Henry Maine.

It should not be forgotten that freedom of contract in practice resulted in anything but real freedom for the vast bulk of the community. "What the Polish Lords called liberty," Lord Acton tells us, "was the right of each of them to veto the acts of the Diet, and to persecute the peasants on his estate." The same may well be said about contractual freedom in our own system. What the opponents of regulatory legislation called liberty was too often the right of the employer to exploit his workers. Unrestricted freedom of contract led to the degradations, the slums, the miseries of the many—compared with the wealth and power of the few.

It may be said of the society of half a century ago what was once aptly said of Kant—that it forgot the ethical whole in its solicitude for the perfection of the parts. If, today, the Constitution is construed to permit limitations upon the contractual freedom of the individual in the abstract, it does so in the interest of insuring that the bulk of the community in the concrete will not be denied the means required for proper human existence. Abstract liberty, in Burke's famous phrase, like other mere abstractions, is not to be found. In a very real sense, the true liberty of the individual may be promoted by restrictions that the society imposes upon him in his own interest.

If the Maine generalization has ceased to be an accurate description of contemporary legal development, it may be because the law has been transforming the very concepts of contract and status. The abstract autonomy of the individual will is no longer the fulcrum upon which the due process clause turns. But most individuals are today freer than they have ever been to make the decisions that count in life. Modern law has, in large part, diminished or removed the status barriers that relentlessly confined people within their class, race, religion, or sex. The ordinary individual in this country enjoys a legal freedom of movement never before attained in the history of civilization. A Constitution construed to authorize such attainment is hardly the basic charter of a society in a state of retrogression.

BIBLIOGRAPHICAL NOTE

THE NOTED FRENCH HISTORIAN Fustel de Coulanges is said to have told a lecture audience "Do not imagine you are listening to me: it is history itself that speaks." The same assertion could hardly be made by the present writer. To one who has read this volume it is scarcely necessary to concede that it is in the main a subjective survey of American constitutional history. It is written from the author's personal point of view and emphasizes those aspects in the constitutional development of the nation which are to him of primary significance.

The same is true of this bibliographical note. Instead of an exhaustive survey of works which are relevant to the constitutional history of the United States (which, in the broadest sense, would include all areas of American history and works relating to them), the author has thought it worthwhile to indicate those books which were of particular value or interest to him in the writing of this volume.

Among general constitutional histories, the most useful are: McLaughlin, Andrew C., *A Constitutional History of the United States* (1935); Swisher, Carl B., *American Constitutional Development* (2nd ed., 1954); Kelly, Alfred H., and Winifred A. Harbison, *The American Constitution, Its Origins and Development* (rev. ed., 1955).

Mention may also be made of Hockett, Homer C., *The Constitutional History of the United States,* Vol. I, *The Blessings of Liberty, 1776–1826;* Vol. II, *A More Perfect Union, 1826–1876* (1939).

In many ways the best treatment of American constitutional history is contained in Warren, Charles, *The Supreme Court in United States History,* three volumes (1922), which on its face is not a constitutional history at all but only a history of the highest American Court. However, as a detailed and intensely readable account of that institution, which is the vital center of the American constitutional system, it covers most of the important areas of our constitutional development. Other historical accounts of the Supreme Court may also be mentioned, notably: Haines, Charles G., *The Role of the Supreme Court in American Government and Politics, 1789–1835* (1961); Haines, Charles G., and Foster H. Sherwood, *The Role of the Supreme Court in American Government and Politics, 1835–1864* (1957); McCloskey, Robert G., *The American Supreme Court* (1960); Schwartz, Bernard, *The Supreme Court: Constitutional Revolution in Retrospect* (1957).

Of particular interest to one concerned with our constitutional history are the great commentaries which have not only explained but also significantly molded American constitutional law. Of these the most important are: Story, Joseph, *Commentaries on the Constitution of the United States,* three volumes (1833); Kent, James, *Commentaries on American Law,* four volumes (1826–1830); Cooley, Thomas M., *A Treatise on the Constitutional Limitations Which Rest Upon the Legislative Power of the States of the American Union* (1868).

During the present century the nearest equivalents (though nowhere near as consequential in their impact upon American law) have been: Willoughby, Westel W., *The Constitutional Law of the United States,* three volumes (2nd ed., 1929); Corwin, Edward S., *The Constitution of the United States of America, Analysis and Interpretation* (1953).

The present writer has recently published the first part of a comprehensive commentary on the Constitution. It is entitled *A Commentary on the Constitution of the United States;* Part One, *The Powers of Government,* Vol. I, *Federal and State Powers,* Vol. II, *The Powers of the President* (1963). Future volumes of this work will deal with the rights of the individual.

Works covering particular periods which were found of especial value include: *Colonial and Revolutionary periods*—Boorstin, Daniel, *The Americans: The Colonial Experience* (1958); Becker, Carl, *The Declaration of Independence* (1942), and *The Eve of the Revolution* (1918); Gipson, L. H., *The Coming of the Revolution, 1763–1775* (1954); McIlwain, Charles H., *The American Revolution: A Constitutional Interpretation* (1958); Miller, John C., *Origins of the American Revolution* (1959); Morgan, Edmund, and Helen M. Morgan, *The Stamp Act Crisis: Prologue to Revolution* (1953), and *The Birth of the Republic, 1763–1789* (1956); Rossiter, Clinton, *Seedtime of the Republic; the Origin of the American Tradition of Political Liberty* (1953); Savelle, Max, *Seeds of Liberty: Genesis of the American Mind* (1948); Van Tyne, C. H., *The Causes of the War of Independence* (1922); Wright, Esmond, *The Fabric of Freedom, 1763–1800* (1961).

The Confederation and making of the Constitution—Jensen, Merrill, *The Articles of Confederation; An Interpretation of the Social-Constitutional History of the American Revolution, 1774–1781* (2nd ed., 1959); McLaughlin, Andrew C., *The Confederation and the Constitution, 1783–1789* (1905); Beard, Charles A., *An Economic Interpretation of the Constitution of the United States* (1935); Farrand, Max, *The Framing of the Constitution of the United States* (1913); Warren, Charles, *The Making of the Constitution* (1929); Rodell, Fred, *Fifty-five Men* (1936); Van Doren, Carl, *The Great Rehearsal* (1948).

The basic source books for the Constitution-making period are: Farrand, Max, *The Records of the Federal Convention of 1787,* four volumes (1937); Elliot, Jonathan, *The Debates in the Several State Conventions on the Adoption of the Federal Consti-*

tution, five volumes (1836–1859); as well as the *Federalist* (published in innumerable editions).

From Marshall to the eve of the Civil War—Of the greatest value here are the now classic biographies: Beveridge, Albert J., *John Marshall,* four volumes (1916–1919); Corwin, Edward S., *John Marshall and the Constitution* (1919); as well as Swisher, Carl B., *Roger B. Taney* (1961).

Other especially useful works on the period are: Dangerfield, George, *Era of Good Feelings* (1953); Van Deusen, G. G., *The Jacksonian Era, 1828–1848* (1959); Schlesinger, Arthur M., Jr., *The Age of Jackson* (1945); Wiltse, Charles, *The New Nation, 1800–1845* (1935).

Civil War and Reconstruction—Of especial interest to the writer were: Randall, J. G., *Constitutional Problems under Lincoln* (rev. ed., 1951); Dunning, William A., *Reconstruction, Political and Economic: 1865–1877* (1907); Woodward, C. Vann, *Origins of the New South, 1877–1913* (1951), and *The Strange Career of Jim Crow* (rev. ed., 1958); Nichols, Roy F., *The Stakes of Power: 1845–1877* (1961).

Modern period—Of particular value to the author were the following: Frankfurter, Felix, *The Commerce Clause under Marshall, Taney and Waite* (1937); Fairman, Charles, *Mr. Justice Miller and the Supreme Court, 1862–1890* (1939); Swisher, Carl B., *Stephen J. Field, Craftsman of the Law* (1930); James, Joseph B., *The Framing of the Fourteenth Amendment* (1956); Fairman, Charles, and Stanley Morrison, "Does the Fourteenth Amendment Incorporate the Bill of Rights?" *2 Stanford Law Review 5, 140* (1949); Corwin, Edward S., *Commerce Power versus States Rights* (1959), *Twilight of the Supreme Court: A History of Our Constitutional Theory* (1934), *Constitutional Revolution, Limited* (1941), and *The President: Office and Powers, 1787–1957* (4th rev. ed., 1957); Twiss, Benjamin R., *Lawyers and the Constitution: How Laissez-Faire Came to the Supreme Court* (1962); Lerner, Max, ed., *The Mind and Faith of Justice Holmes* (1943); Mason, Alpheus T., *Brandeis: A Free Man's Life* (1956), and *Harlan Fiske Stone: Pillar of the Law* (1956); Pusey, Merlo J., *Charles Evans Hughes,* two volumes

(1951); Jackson, Robert H., *The Struggle for Judicial Supremacy* (1941), and *The Supreme Court in the American System of Government* (1955).

Mention should also be made of two recent works which have greatly stimulated those interested in constitutional development: Neustadt, Richard E., *Presidential Power, The Politics of Leadership* (1960); Burns, James M., *The Deadlock of Democracy; Four-Party Politics in America* (1963).

The discussion at the end of the last chapter was greatly influenced by the writings of Roscoe Pound, particularly his massive *Jurisprudence,* five volumes (1959), and Wolfgang Friedmann, particularly his *Law in a Changing Society* (1959).

INDEX